First World War
and Army of Occupation
War Diary
France, Belgium and Germany

23 DIVISION
68 Infantry Brigade,
Brigade Machine Gun Company
13 December 1915 - 31 October 1917

WO95/2182/5

The Naval & Military Press Ltd
www.nmarchive.com
Published in association with The National Archives

Published by

The Naval & Military Press Ltd

Unit 10 Ridgewood Industrial Park,

Uckfield, East Sussex,

TN22 5QE England

Tel: +44 (0) 1825 749494

www.naval-military-press.com

www.nmarchive.com

This diary has been reprinted in facsimile from the original. Any imperfections are inevitably reproduced and the quality may fall short of modern type and cartographic standards.

© **Crown Copyright**
Images reproduced by permission of The National Archives, London, England, 2015.

Contents

Document type	Place/Title	Date From	Date To
Heading	WO95/2182/5 Inf 68 Bde M.G. Coy. Dec 1915-Oct 1917		
Heading	23rd Division 68th Infy Bde 68th Machine Gun Coy. Dec 1915-1917 Oct To Italy.		
Heading	68 M G Coy Vol 1 Dec 15. Mar 18		
War Diary	Grantham	13/12/1915	23/02/1916
War Diary	Le Havre	25/02/1916	03/03/1916
War Diary	Bruay	04/03/1916	04/03/1916
War Diary	Calonne	05/03/1916	05/03/1916
War Diary	Ricquart	08/03/1916	09/03/1916
War Diary	Fresnicourt	10/03/1916	16/03/1916
War Diary	Hersin	17/03/1916	17/03/1916
War Diary	Calonne Sector Trenche	17/03/1916	31/03/1916
War Diary	Calonne Sector Trenches	18/03/1916	17/04/1916
War Diary	Calonne Sector Trenches	02/04/1916	17/04/1916
War Diary	Hersin	19/04/1916	26/04/1916
War Diary	Beugin	26/04/1916	30/04/1916
War Diary	Beugin.	26/04/1916	30/04/1916
War Diary	Beugin.	01/04/1916	30/04/1916
Miscellaneous	To D.A.G. 3rd Echelon	03/06/1916	03/06/1916
War Diary	Beugin	01/05/1916	04/05/1916
War Diary	Beugin.	02/05/1916	04/05/1916
War Diary	Vincly	05/05/1916	15/05/1916
War Diary	Fosse 7	15/05/1916	16/05/1916
War Diary	Souchey 2. Sector	16/05/1916	31/05/1916
War Diary	Aix Noulette	01/06/1916	09/06/1916
War Diary	Aix Noulette.	08/06/1916	08/06/1916
War Diary	Bouvigny	09/06/1916	09/06/1916
War Diary	Notre Dame	10/06/1916	12/06/1916
War Diary	Bouvigny	13/06/1916	13/06/1916
War Diary	La Thieuloye	14/06/1916	14/06/1916
War Diary	Bergueneuse	15/06/1916	15/06/1916
War Diary	Vincly	15/06/1916	22/06/1916
War Diary	Vincly.	18/06/1916	23/06/1916
War Diary	Delette	24/06/1916	24/06/1916
War Diary	St Pierre	25/06/1916	26/06/1916
War Diary	Brielly	27/06/1916	30/06/1916
War Diary	Vincly	17/06/1916	17/06/1916
Heading	68th Bde. 23rd Div. War Diary Brigade temporarily under Orders of 34th Division 16th to 20th July. 68th Machine Gun Company. July 1916		
War Diary	Franvillers	01/07/1916	01/07/1916
War Diary	Millencourt	02/07/1916	02/07/1916
War Diary	Albert	04/07/1916	05/07/1916
War Diary	Becourt Wood & Trenches.	06/07/1916	10/07/1916
War Diary	Albert	11/07/1916	14/07/1916
War Diary	Becourt Wood	15/07/1916	16/07/1916
War Diary	Trenches	17/07/1916	19/07/1916
War Diary	Albert	20/07/1916	20/07/1916
War Diary	Franvillers	21/07/1916	26/07/1916

War Diary	Trenches	26/07/1916	28/07/1916
War Diary	Albert	29/07/1916	31/07/1916
Heading	68th Brigade. 23rd Division. 68th Brigade Machine Gun Company August 1916		
War Diary	Trenches	29/07/1916	05/08/1916
War Diary	Trenches.	03/08/1916	05/08/1916
War Diary	Albert	06/08/1916	08/08/1916
War Diary	Behencourt	09/08/1916	11/08/1916
War Diary	Gorenflos	12/08/1916	13/08/1916
War Diary	Thieushouk	14/08/1916	15/08/1916
War Diary	Trenches	16/08/1916	31/08/1916
War Diary	Trenches Bailleul	01/09/1916	05/09/1916
War Diary	Westrove	06/09/1916	10/09/1916
War Diary	Molliens	10/09/1916	12/09/1916
War Diary	Millencourt	13/09/1916	14/09/1916
War Diary	Becourt Wood	15/09/1916	17/09/1916
War Diary	Contalmaison	18/09/1916	22/09/1916
War Diary	Trenches	23/09/1916	01/10/1916
War Diary	Contalmaison	02/10/1916	02/10/1916
War Diary	Before Le Sars.	02/10/1916	30/11/1916
War Diary		01/11/1916	30/11/1916
War Diary	Erie Camp	01/12/1916	05/12/1916
War Diary	Trenches Ypres	06/12/1916	22/12/1916
War Diary	Camp	23/12/1916	29/12/1916
War Diary	Trenches Ypres	30/12/1916	01/01/1917
Heading	Confidential. War Diary Of No 68 Company Machine Gun Corps from 1st January 1917 to 1st February 1917. Vol XI.		
War Diary	Trenches Ypres	01/01/1917	15/01/1917
War Diary	Eyrie Camp	16/01/1917	24/01/1917
War Diary	Trenches Ypres	25/01/1917	31/01/1917
Heading	Confidential. War Diary of No. 68 Company Machine Gun Corps from 1st February 1917. to 1st March. 1917. Vol 12		
War Diary	In The Trenches Ypres	01/02/1917	07/02/1917
War Diary	Eyrie Camp	08/02/1917	15/02/1917
War Diary	Trench Ypres	16/02/1917	26/02/1917
War Diary	Camp S	27/02/1917	28/02/1917
Heading	War Diary March 1917. No. 68 Company Machine Gun Corps. Vol 13		
War Diary	Merckeghem	01/03/1917	20/03/1917
War Diary	'Y' Camp	21/03/1917	21/03/1917
War Diary	'S' Camp	22/03/1917	31/03/1917
Heading	War Diary of No. 68 Coy. Machine Gun Corps from 1st April, 1917 to 30th April 1917. Vol.4		
War Diary	Comp 'S'	01/04/1917	04/04/1917
War Diary	Merckeghem	05/04/1917	13/04/1917
War Diary	Abeele	13/03/1917	13/03/1917
War Diary	Erie Camp	14/04/1917	14/04/1917
War Diary	Abeele	14/04/1917	14/04/1917
War Diary	In Trenches	15/04/1917	30/04/1917
Heading	War Diary from 1st May 1917. to 31st May. 1917. No. 68 Coy. Machine Gun Corps. 3-6-1917. Vol 15		
War Diary	Ypres	01/05/1917	01/05/1917
War Diary	Steenvoorde	02/05/1917	09/05/1917
War Diary	Winnipeg Camp	10/05/1917	11/05/1917

War Diary	In The Trenches	12/05/1917	19/05/1917
War Diary	Winnipeg Camp	20/05/1917	23/05/1917
War Diary	In Trenches	24/05/1917	29/05/1917
War Diary	Dominion Lines	30/05/1917	30/05/1917
War Diary	M. Camp	31/05/1917	31/05/1917
Heading	War Diary of No. 68 Coy. Machine Gun Corps From 1st June 1917 to 30th June 1917. Vol 16		
War Diary	Trenches Hill 60 Sector	01/06/1917	15/06/1917
War Diary	Nr Thieshouk	16/06/1917	29/06/1917
War Diary	Zevecoten Camp	30/06/1917	30/06/1917
Heading	War Diary of No. 68. Company Machine Gun Corps From 1st July 1917 To 31st July 1917. Vol 17		
War Diary	Zevecoten Camp	01/07/1917	05/07/1917
War Diary	Mount Sorrel Hill 60 Sector	06/07/1916	31/07/1916
Heading	War Diary of No. 68 Company Machine Gun Corps. From Aug 1st 1917 to Aug 31st 1917. Vol 18		
War Diary	Esquerdes	01/08/1917	08/08/1917
War Diary	Salperwick	09/08/1917	31/08/1917
Heading	War Diary of No. 68 Coy. M.G.C. From Sept 1st 1917 To Sept 30th 1917. Vol 19		
War Diary	Dickebush Area	01/09/1917	03/09/1917
War Diary	Steenvoorde Area	04/09/1917	04/09/1917
War Diary	Noordpeene	05/09/1917	13/09/1917
War Diary	Steenvoorde	14/09/1917	14/09/1917
War Diary	Chippewa Camp	15/09/1917	16/09/1917
War Diary	Dickebush	17/09/1917	19/09/1917
War Diary	Trenches	20/09/1917	25/09/1917
War Diary	Westoutre	26/09/1917	30/09/1917
Miscellaneous	Second Army Offensive Brigade Plan Of Operations. Appendix "A".		
Miscellaneous	Company H.Q. at Torr Top. Action of No 4 Section. Appendix "B".		
Miscellaneous	Programme for 'I' and "J" Batteries. Appendix "B".		
Miscellaneous	Corrigenda To Brigade Instruction No. 1 Plan Of Operations.		
Miscellaneous	Machine Guns.		
Miscellaneous	Artillery Arrangements.		
War Diary	Action of No 2 Section.		
Map			
Heading	No 68 Coy. M.G.C. Confidential War Diary From Oct 1st 1917 to Oct 31st 1917. Vol 20		
War Diary	Thieushouck	01/10/1917	07/10/1917
War Diary	Westoutre	08/10/1917	31/10/1917

WO95/2182/5

Int
68 Bde MG Coy

Dec 1915 - Oct 1917

23RD DIVISION
68TH INFY BDE

68TH MACHINE GUN COY.

DEC 1915 - MAR 1916.

1917 OCT

TO ITALY

23RD DIVISION
68TH INFY BDE

23

68 M6 Coy
Vol 1

Dec 15
Nov 18

Army Form C. 2118.

WAR DIARY
or
INTELLIGENCE SUMMARY.
(Erase heading not required.)

Instructions regarding War Diaries and Intelligence Summaries are contained in F.S. Regs, Part II. and the Staff Manual respectively. Title pages will be prepared in manuscript.

No. 1

Place	Date	Hour	Summary of Events and Information	Remarks and references to Appendices
	1915			
Grantham	13 Dec	2 pm	Company formed – Strength officers & [crossed out] 141 other ranks.	SR
"	14 Dec to 22.2.16		Progressive instruction carried out in Machine gun work – Sgts & 22 O.R. Course of instruction in transport duties at various Centres – administration work – Coy Comdr found much of his time taken up with administration work owing to insufficient staff – No orderly room clerk is allowed in establishment – 2 hr for water duties added to Estⁿ	SR
Grantham	23.2.16	12.15 am	Left Camp & Entrained – Company composed of every detail – Embarked Southampton on S.S. Marguerite. 6 officers. 115 other ranks. The Transport, with 3 officers & 31 other ranks embarked on S.S. Archimedes – about 7 pm	SR
Le Havre	25.2.16	7a–	Dis-embarked from S.S. Marguerite, and marched to Camp 5 – under canvas	SR
"	26.2.16	9a–	Marched to Camp 2.	
"	26.2.16 to 2.3.16		S.S. Archimedes did not arrive until 2nd March – Intervening time used for such instruction as was possible – Drawing further stores from ordnance & routine work	SR
"	2.3.16		S.S. Archimedes arrives – Transport unloaded – Accident to one limber its contents & wheel fell into hold of ship, causing damage to contents – due to sling breaking.	SR
"	3.3.16	9am	Board of Enquiry re damaged stores – Accident due to the bad condition of tackle used for unloading by shore authorities – Left about 5.40 by train for –	SR

Army Form C. 2118.

WAR DIARY
or
INTELLIGENCE SUMMARY.
(Erase heading not required.)

Instructions regarding War Diaries and Intelligence Summaries are contained in F. S. Regs., Part II. and the Staff Manual respectively. Title pages will be prepared in manuscript.

No 2

Place	Date	Hour	Summary of Events and Information	Remarks and references to Appendices
	March 1916			
Bruay	4th	3 PM	Arrived BRUAY. Conducted & reported to Brigade Head Quarters. Went into billets at Calonne	See
Calonne	5th		Training in Machine Gun work - Care of ammunition Horses etc. Much discussion Reading of orders	See
Ricquart	8th		G.O.C's inspection. 2 PM 6th Should have moved in the 8th but move postponed to 9th	See
"	9th	8 am	Marched to other billets at FRESNICOURT - Men in huts erected by French. Very dirty, necessitating	See
			much cleaning - Tried all our guns - Found them in good order	
Fresnicourt	10th		Continued training - Officers visit trenches where we expected to take over. Route march -	See
	15th		Orders to again change billets, advanced billets party leave on 15th inst. 2nd R.H. Brigade	
	16th	8.30 a	Marched to other billets at HERSIN. Visited new line of trenches at CALONNE	See
			Sector 1 made arrangements to take over from 60 Brigade	
Hersin	17th	3 pm	Moved forward billetting our at FOSSE 10. Took over trenches at 7 PM.	
			Eight guns in front line, 2 in support, 6 in reserve. Meaning 10 gun the	
			manner contemplated - Considerable difficulty in arranging relief owing	
			to the establishment being not allowing for casualties - on the	
			whole we were waiting for Reinforcement when 9 other men turning up	See
			in hospital - Our establishment showed certainly to be in excess by 20 or so	

Army Form C. 2118.

WAR DIARY
or
INTELLIGENCE SUMMARY.
(Erase heading not required.)

No 3

Instructions regarding War Diaries and Intelligence Summaries are contained in F. S. Regs., Part II. and the Staff Manual respectively. Title pages will be prepared in manuscript.

Place	Date	Hour	Summary of Events and Information	Remarks and references to Appendices
CALONNE SECTOR TRENCHES	March 1916 17th to 31st		Continued to hold guns as shown before. Relief every 48 hours. The work carried on same day as infantry. Improved & added emplacements – materials for pivot & chequespears mountings sent in. Artillery active. M. Gun Chiefly active fire against working parties in the evenings. Very little movement observed in enemy trenches. Fire in some instances directed against aeroplanes, with no result so far as could (?) except on one (?) when our fire caused an enemy plane to return in direction of our line.	
	18th	3 a.m.	Two guns of Right Section dispersed with several casualties, working parties of about 25 enemy.	B
		8 a.m.	Left Sectn (1 gun) fired at Otto Post in Salient	A
	26th	2 p.m.	Four guns took part in Bde minor operation. During the period the only casualties have been one to mens alloted – many narrow escapes. One gun damaged by shell fire but did not prevent its firing. The company is composed very largely of young soldiers whose adaptability to the work is excellent & their conduct generally is I think wonderfully good.	A

[Signature] Capt
Comdg No 5 Coy, Machine Gun Corps

[Stamp: No 5 COMPANY 31 MAR 1916 MACHINE GUN CORPS]

Army Form C. 2118.

No. 4

WAR DIARY
or
INTELLIGENCE SUMMARY.
(Erase heading not required.)

Instructions regarding War Diaries and Intelligence Summaries are contained in F. S. Regs., Part II. and the Staff Manual respectively. Title pages will be prepared in manuscript.

Place	Date	Hour	Summary of Events and Information	Remarks and references to Appendices
CALONNE SECTOR TRENCHES	April 1st 6&7 17		Continued to keep 8 guns in front line and two in support and six in reserve. During this period a considerable amount of movement in enemies lines was observed	WA
	2 April	1 a.m.	1 Gun on Right Sector fired about 100 rounds at a working party of about 60 strong who appeared to be digging. The party was dispersed and judging by the cries that were heard must have suffered several casualties. The gun was fired from the parapet 80 yards to the left of the emplacement	WA
	3 April	9.30 p.m.	A large German working party was observed on the Right Sector. Machine Gun fire was opened in co-operation with a Lewis Gun. The party dispersed with some celerity and sentries at the cap head were of the opinion that the shots were right amongst them	WA
	4 April	9.45	1 Gun of Right Sector dispersed two small enemies working parties. Result unknown	WA
	5 April	9 p.m.	1 Gun of Right Sector fired about 500 rounds on the enemys parapet from the alternative emplacement to support an attempt to blow in a saphead. 1 Lewis gun cooperated	WA

Army Form C. 2118.

WAR DIARY
or
INTELLIGENCE SUMMARY.
(Erase heading not required.)

No. 5

Place	Date	Hour	Summary of Events and Information	Remarks and references to Appendices
CALONNE SECTOR TRENCHES	5 April	10.30 p.m.	1 Gun of Right Sect'n fired at an enemy working party which was at work. The party were heard and not seen and it is believed the enemy's party suffered casualties.	WA
	6 April	8.30 p.m	On Left Sect'n an enemy's patrol was observed on left of railway 1 gun opened fire and the patrol was seen running in the direction of their line leaving 6 dead and it is believed that of the others who returned to their own lines some were wounded	WA
	8 April	11 p.m.	4 Guns of Right Sect'n in co-operation with 6 Lewis Guns laid on enemy's sap and fired about 50 rounds per gun	WA
	10 April	10 p.m	1 Gun of Right Sect'n fired about 180 rounds at 3 working parties. It is not known if any were hit	WA
	12 April	8.30 p.m	1 Gun of Right Sect'n fired about 40 rounds at a small patrol or working party and dispersed them	WA
	10 April	4.30	All guns on front line (8) harried the enemy's parapet, two taking part in a Brigade Scheme	WA
	17 April	10.45	Relieved from trenches by the 6th Brigade Machine Gun Company. Relief completed by 16.45	WA

Army Form C. 2118.

No. 6

WAR DIARY
or
INTELLIGENCE SUMMARY.
(Erase heading not required.)

Instructions regarding War Diaries and Intelligence Summaries are contained in F. S. Regs., Part II. and the Staff Manual respectively. Title pages will be prepared in manuscript.

Place	Date	Hour	Summary of Events and Information	Remarks and references to Appendices
CALONNE SECTOR TRENCHES	1 April to 17 April	-	During this period Muzzle Pivot Mountings were fitted in all battle emplacements. Casualties during period 1-17 April 2 men wounded and 2 wounded at duty.	WA
Bruay	19 April to 26 April		Programme of work carried out during this period:— 1. Mechanism and elementary Machine Gun work for Drivers and men recently joined and a few backward men. 2. Riding and horsemanship for Officers and remainder of Company 3. Standing of arms, saluting, march and billet discipline for everyone 4. Improvement of stables 5. Packing and unpacking limbers During this period the G.O.C. Division inspected the Company. Left Hersin about 10 a.m and marched to new Billets at Bruay arriving about 1.30 p.m.	WA WA WA WA WA WA
Bruay	26 April to 30 April		Programme of work carried out during this period:— Drivers continue Mechanism, Immediate action and Gun Drill. Men under instruction in Horsemanship continue. Riding Driving Limbers	WA WA

T/134. Wt. W708-776. 50(000. 4/15. Sir J. C. & S.

Army Form C. 2118.

No. 7

WAR DIARY
or
INTELLIGENCE SUMMARY.
(Erase heading not required.)

Instructions regarding War Diaries and Intelligence Summaries are contained in F.S. Regs., Part II. and the Staff Manual respectively. Title pages will be prepared in manuscript.

Place	Date	Hour	Summary of Events and Information	Remarks and references to Appendices
Bergen	26 to 30 April		Putting together and cleaning harness, grooming and care of animals. All the Company - Handling of Arms - Saluting - Physical Training. Route March - Simple tactical scheme. Rangefinding - Special instruction. Sanitary Squad - Instruction in sanitary duties, especially of a unit on the move.	W/A
				W/A
	1 April to 17 April		During this period we found great difficulties in finding the necessary reliefs for the guns on account of some of our men being admitted to hospital.	W/A
	18 to 30 April		During this period training has been carried on, and it seems to have done the men a lot of good, although hard worked on account of the establishment being so small, they seem to have taken a great interest in their work. The conduct of the men is so excellent.	W/A
			Note:- The establishment does not include any orderly room staff, this is very necessary - We are allowed 1 Cold Shoer, this is inadequate. A travelling kitchen would be a great help. The fuel issued would appear to be on the	W/A

T2134. Wt. W708-776. 500,000. 4/16. Sir J. C. & S.

WAR DIARY
or
INTELLIGENCE SUMMARY.
(Erase heading not required.)

Army Form C. 2118.

No. 8

Place	Date	Hour	Summary of Events and Information	Remarks and references to Appendices
Beuvry			assumption that we have one of these. We are allowed no spare animals to replace casualties, whereas I believe other units have about 10 per cent. The baggage wagon is always with the Supply Company A.S.C. for the purpose of carrying rations and forage and I suggest it would greatly add to the efficiency of the unit if an extra G.S. Wagon was added to the establishment, no so any provision made for Officers Mess material, there are now 10 Officers in the establishment, and if a travelling cooker were provided for the men the present cooks cart, which is really an Officers Mess cart could be utilyed for this purpose. As regards the establishment I consider it necessary that the number of men should be increased to 200, only by such increase can one hope to attain the standard of efficiency desired.	WH.

H. Harmon 2/Lt
(COMDG. No. 68 COY. MACHINE GUN CORPS)

2o.

D.A.G
3rd Echelon.

[Stamp: No. 4 COMPANY MACHINE GUN CORPS — 3 JUN 1916]

Herewith War Diary for month of May please.

W. Harrison 2Lt
COMDG. No. 6 COY. MACHINE GUN CORPS

62 M G Coy
Army Form C. 2118.
XXIII   No 9 Vol 3

WAR DIARY
or
INTELLIGENCE SUMMARY.
(Erase heading not required.)

Place	Date	Hour	Summary of Events and Information	Remarks and references to Appendices
Bergun	1-5-16 to 4-5-16		The following training carried out during this period:- Physical training, Packing and Cleaning of Limbers, Cleaning of Rifles, Tactical Handling, Manoeuvre of ground and methods of advance, and Re-shoeing of Limber wagon wheels	W.H.
	2-5-16	3 p.m.	Inspected by G.O.C. First Army	W.H.
	4-5-16		Preparing for move to new training area	W.H.
Vincly	5-5-16	2.30	Left Bergun at 6 a.m. and marched to Vincly arriving about 2.30 p.m. - No casualties on the line of march.	W.H.
Vincly	6-5-16 to 15-5-16		The following training was carried out during this period, and consequently much progress was made in the Company	W.H.
	6-5-16		Taking up positions (Sections independently)	W.H.
	7-5-16		Sections in attack (Advance and Rearguards)	W.H.
	8-5-16		1/2 Companys in attack (working against each other)	W.H.
	9-5-16		Company in attack (Covering fire)	W.H.
	10-5-16		Company in attack (Rearguard action)	W.H.
	11-5-16		Brigade scheme - attack	W.H.
	12-5-16		Company in attack (Defensive line and outposts day and night)	W.H.

Army Form C. 2118.

No. 10.

WAR DIARY
or
INTELLIGENCE SUMMARY.
(Erase heading not required.)

Instructions regarding War Diaries and Intelligence Summaries are contained in F. S. Regs., Part II. and the Staff Manual respectively. Title pages will be prepared in manuscript.

Place	Date	Hour	Summary of Events and Information	Remarks and references to Appendices
Vimy	13-5-16		Brigade in attack – Defensive line and outposts	WA
	14-5-16		Brigade scheme – Rearguard	WA
	6-5-16		During this period the following daily training was carried out:	
	15-5-16		Horsemanship. Saluting. Musketry, Drill, Routine Machine Gun work.	WA
			Map reading and Lectures on Machine Gun work	WA
Zone 7	15-5-16		Left training area and marched to new area arriving about 4 p.m.	WA
	16-5-16		Relieved No. 24 Machine Gun Company from trenches. Relief completed by 12 – midnight.	WA
Souchez 2 Sector	16-5-16 to 31-5-16		Eight guns in front line and eight in reserve. Continued to keep 8 guns in front line and 8 in reserve – Reliefs carried out every 5 days. Two awards relieving on same day as infantry – During this period very little movement detected in enemy trenches – On the night of the 22nd a large enemy shell blew in the back of one of the emplacements wounding 5463 Cpl King and breaking his leg – In spite of many shells bursting very near the emplacement Cpl King with fine regard to duty was cleaning the emplacement of ammunition etc when he received his wound having just previously carried the gun to a place of safety in the dug out – The gun would	

WAR DIARY
or
INTELLIGENCE SUMMARY.
(Erase heading not required.)

Army Form C. 2118.

Nº 11.

Place	Date	Hour	Summary of Events and Information	Remarks and references to Appendices
SOUCHEZ Sectn (contd)	16.5.16 3.3.16	5a	have been destroyed if it had not been removed by Col King in face of this intense high explosive shell fire for which eventually wounded him — In this particular front very few dug outs and emplacements have been made consequently much work has been done in front and support lines digging dug outs and making and improving emplacements — During the period 8 men per battalion of Brigade have been attached to this Company for duty this it makes things much easier to work and allows the men a little more rest — The conduct of the men is quite good.	WA. WA.

68 M. Coy
Vol 4
12 June

Army Form C. 2118.

WAR DIARY
or
INTELLIGENCE SUMMARY.
(Erase heading not required.)

Place	Date	Hour	Summary of Events and Information	Remarks and references to Appendices
AIX NOULETTE	1 JUNE 1916		Continued to keep 8 guns in reserve at AIX NOULETTE – During this period very little movement was noticed on enemies lines – In this particular part of the line very few dug outs and emplacements have been made consequently much work has been done in front and support lines digging dug outs and making and improving emplacements –	N/A
	8 JUNE 1916		Relieved by 69 Machine Gun Company in SOUCHEZ SECTOR This company relieving	N/A
BOUVIGNY	9 JUNE 1916		69 Machine Gun Company in NOTRE DAME – Relief completed 2AM 10 June	N/A
NOTRE DAME	10 JUNE 1916		8 guns in reserve line – The remaining 8 guns were left in Divisional Reserve at HERSIN. Company Head Quarters at BOUVIGNY.	N/A
"	12 JUNE 1916		Relieved by 141 Machine Gun Company – Relief completed by 3AM	N/A
BOUVIGNY	13 JUNE 1916		Moved from BOUVIGNY and marched to LA THIEULOYE – Billeted for night Arrived in village about 3P.M. Casualties on the line of march nil –	N/A
LA THIEULOYE	14 JUNE 1916		Left LA THIEULOYE at 7a.m. and marched to BERGUENEUSE – Billeted for night Arrived in village about 2p.m. Casualties on the line of march nil	N/A
BERGUENEUSE	15 JUNE 1916		Left BERGUENEUSE about 10A.M. and marched to VINCLY. Arrived in village about 1.30p.m. Casualties on the line of march nil –	N/A

Army Form C. 2118.

WAR DIARY
or
INTELLIGENCE SUMMARY.
(Erase heading not required.)

Instructions regarding War Diaries and Intelligence Summaries are contained in F. S. Regs., Part II. and the Staff Manual respectively. Title pages will be prepared in manuscript.

Place	Date	Hour	Summary of Events and Information	Remarks and references to Appendices
VINCLY	15 June 1916 to 22 June 1916		During this period much progress was made and training carried out as follows: 1. Physical Training 2. Mechanism 3. Gun Drill 4. Handling of Arms 5. Saluting 6. Packing & Cleaning Limbers 7. Grooming & care of animals 8. Putting together and cleaning harness. 9. Simple tactical schemes 10. Firing	WH
"	18 June 1916		Brigade Scheme	WH
"	20 June 1916		Divisional Scheme	WH
"	23 June 1916		Left VINCLY and marched to DELETTE. Billeted for night.	WH
DELETTE	24 June 1916		Left DELETTE 3AM and marched to AIRE STATION arriving about 7AM. Entrained at AIRE STATION for AMIENS arriving about 5.30 PM. Detrained at a siding near AMIENS and marched to billets at ST PIERRE arriving in billets about 1AM.	WH
ST PIERRE	25 June 1916		Training carried out as follows:- 1. Packing and cleaning limbers	
"	26 June 1916		2. Grooming and care of animals 3. Putting together and cleaning harness 4. Route march	WH
"	26 June 1916		Left ST PIERRE 9.30 PM and marched to BRIELLY arriving 11.15 PM in billets.	WH

WAR DIARY or INTELLIGENCE SUMMARY.

Army Form C. 2118.

Place	Date	Hour	Summary of Events and Information	Remarks and references to Appendices
BRIELLY	27 June 1916 to 30 June 1916		During this period the following training carried out:- 1 Physical Training 2 Route March 3 Simple tactical schemes.-	WA
VINCLY	17 June 1916		Inspected by G.O.C. Machine Gun Corps -	WA
			5468 Cpl. J. King of this Company awarded the MILITARY MEDAL (Authority First Army No 2/461/A.M.S 16/6/16)	WA
			During this month the Company have made steady progress, and the training carried out seems to have made a great improvement in the Company	WA

68th Bde.
23rd Div.

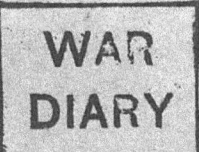
WAR DIARY

Brigade temporarily under orders
of 34th Division 16th to 20th July.

68th MACHINE GUN COMPANY.

JULY 1916.

23/ July

Army Form C. 2118.

68 M.G. Coy /5
Vol 5

WAR DIARY
or
INTELLIGENCE SUMMARY.

(Erase heading not required.)

Instructions regarding War Diaries and Intelligence Summaries are contained in F. S. Regs., Part II. and the Staff Manual respectively. Title pages will be prepared in manuscript.

Place	Date	Hour	Summary of Events and Information	Remarks and references to Appendices
	1916			
FRANVILLERS	1-7-16		Company moved to FRANVILLERS and billed for night	WA
MILLENCOURT	2-7-16		Company moved from FRANVILLERS and marched to MILLENCOURT and bivouaced for 2 days -	WA
ALBERT	4-7-16		Company moved from MILLENCOURT and marched to a field S.W of ALBERT into Bivouac -	WA
"	5-7-16		Company moved into BECOURT WOOD, but returned to the S.W of ALBERT on account of not being required to take over trenches until following day -	WA
BECOURT WOOD	6-7-16		Company moved into BECOURT WOOD - Reconnaissance of ground to be taken over from 69 Bay Machine Gun Coys by O.C Coy and Section Commanders - Relieved 69 Coy M G C in the trenches - Relief commenced at about 2.30 p.m and was completed about 5.30.h.m.	WA
TRENCHES			No 4 Section (4 guns) took up position in front of BIRCH TREE WOOD. No. 3 Section (4 guns) had 2 guns at SCOTS REDOUBT and 2 guns in the TRIANGLE Head Quarters and remaining 2 sections remained at BECOURT with orders to move off at 10 minutes notice	WA
"	7-7-16		Received orders that the Brigade would attack at 8 A.M. Company Head Quarters	

No 20 COMPANY 4-8-16 MACHINE GUN CORPS

Army Form C. 2118.

16.

WAR DIARY
or
INTELLIGENCE SUMMARY.
(Erase heading not required.)

Instructions regarding War Diaries and Intelligence Summaries are contained in F.S. Regs., Part II. and the Staff Manual respectively. Title pages will be prepared in manuscript.

Place	Date	Hour	Summary of Events and Information	Remarks and references to Appendices
BECOURT WOOD	7-7-16		and No 1 Section (4 guns) were moved up in support to ROUND WOOD – No 2 section went to BRIGADE Head Quarters in reserve – Special arrangements were made for supply of ammunition and additional water, food, and oil sent up to gun teams –	WR
9 TRENCHES			RIGHT SECTOR – The attack which was carried out by the 11 Northumberland Fusiliers did not take place until 9.30 A.M. However at 8 A.M. 2 guns were pushed forward in advance of the infantry under Lt WARWICK to PEAKE Wood to bring oblique fire on the objective – As the attack did not develop they were withdrawn when it was learnt that the attack would take place at 9.30 A.M. In the meantime we supported an attack from our right by the 24 Brigade with heavy fire from the 2 guns at BIRCH WOOD some 5000 rounds were fired – At 9.30 A.M 1 gun was again pushed forward to PEAKE WOOD and fired some 1200 rounds at objective – After the attack the gun was withdrawn as there was no infantry in PEAKE WOOD – The remainder of guns on the right searched enemy's communications into CONTALMAISON –	WR
			LEFT SECTOR – The two guns in the TRIANGLE under 2 LT SMITH had been	

T2134. Wt. W708–776. 500000. 4/15. Sir J.C. & S.

Army Form C. 2118.

17

WAR DIARY
or
INTELLIGENCE SUMMARY.
(Erase heading not required.)

Instructions regarding War Diaries and Intelligence Summaries are contained in F. S. Regs., Part II. and the Staff Manual respectively. Title pages will be prepared in manuscript.

Place	Date	Hour	Summary of Events and Information	Remarks and references to Appendices
BECOURT WOOD & TRENCHES.			so placed that they could bring overhead fire to bear on the objective and direct fire on the communications in rear. At 9.30 A.M when the attack by the 11th Northumberland Fusiliers commenced 2500 rounds were fired with good effect. Later in the day one of the guns from SCOTS REDOUBT was moved up to the TRIANGLE to further cover the GAP between 68th and 24th Brigades and to give close support to our infantry.	W.A
"	8-7-16		Weather conditions were particularly bad on night of 7th-8th and the 2 advanced sections having been continuously at work, were relieved by the Section (No 2) in reserve reinforced by drivers, cooks, and some few reinforcements who had arrived late on the 7th. No. 1 Section remained in support at ROUND WOOD. The relief was completed about 4 P.M.	W.A
			RIGHT SECTOR. During the evening support by fire was given to an attack by the 24 Brigade on CONTALMAISON. Later it was reported that the enemy intended to deliver counter attack. One of the support guns was moved up to the right of BIRCH WOOD to cover valley between own right and 24 Brigade who were now holding SHELTER ALLEY.	W.A

Army Form C. 2118.

WAR DIARY
or
INTELLIGENCE SUMMARY.
(Erase heading not required.)

18.

Place	Date	Hour	Summary of Events and Information	Remarks and references to Appendices
BECOURT WOOD & TRENCHES.	9-7-16		LEFT SECTOR. The remaining gun at SCOTS REDOUBT under instructions from Brigade moved forward to cover the left of BAILIFF WOOD. During the day fire was directed at the enemy's communications. The night 8th–9th was uneventful. The day opened with heavy enemy bombardment but no attack followed. Owing to move machine guns being placed on the right sector of 24th Brigade and Motor Machine Gun Service 2 of our guns were withdrawn into support at ROUND WOOD and No 1 Section from ROUND WOOD to BECOURT WOOD for rest. Nos 3 and 4 Sections were again fit to go forward if necessary and were held in readiness to move off. Several targets were found during the day in both sectors. Some 3000 rounds being fired. In the evening arrangements were made to assist the attack by the Durham Light Infantry at 6 P.M. and fire from both flanks was directed against CHATEAU and other points for some reason the attack did not appear to have taken place.	WA
	10-7-16		Notified that the 1st Brigade would relieve us after an attack by 69 Brigade	WA

Army Form C. 2118.

19.

WAR DIARY
or
INTELLIGENCE SUMMARY.
(Erase heading not required.)

Place	Date	Hour	Summary of Events and Information	Remarks and references to Appendices
BECOURT WOOD & TRENCHES	10-7-16		had taken place. Arrangements were made for 7 guns to assist the attack of 69 Brigade but they sent guns of their own for this purpose – They did not wish us to co-operate beyond keeping our guns in readiness in event of anything going wrong – The 1st Brigade arrived BECOURT WOOD at 7.30 P.M and relief commenced but owing to shell fire and organization in the trenches the relief was not completed before early in the morning of the 11th. – During the period we were in action we had 3 men killed, 7 wounded and 7 wounded at duty. We also had 1 gun completely destroyed and 3 others damaged by shell fire – The 3 latter were sufficiently repaired to continue firing until they were replaced – I have nothing but praise for the behaviour of all ranks who acted splendidly under new and trying conditions of warfare and especially when it is considered that practically each gun is an isolated unit throwing much responsibility for its correct employment on the Officer and N.C.O in charge. – During the whole time I was kept well informed by messages of the progress of events and was able to pass them on to other units	W.A.

T.J131.   Wt. W708-776.   50C000.   4/15.   Sir J. C. & S.

Army Form C. 2118.

WAR DIARY
or
INTELLIGENCE SUMMARY.
(Erase heading not required.)

Instructions regarding War Diaries and Intelligence Summaries are contained in F. S. Regs., Part II. and the Staff Manual respectively. Title pages will be prepared in manuscript.

20.

Place	Date	Hour	Summary of Events and Information	Remarks and references to Appendices
BECOURT WOOD			including artillery – Forms giving particulars of act of gallantry were sent in for Corporal Hulett and Pte Rich both of whom showed a complete	WA
" TRENCHES			indifference to danger when their duty necessitated it – Copy of recommendations – 5521 Cpl Hulett during the recent action was twice reported for bravery 1. On the 7th July 1916 a portion of SCOTS REDOUBT trench was so heavily shelled that there was no trench left – It was vacated by all the troops including the gun team who did so under the orders of Cpl Hulett he himself remounted the gun which had been buried proceeded to clean it ready for use although the shelling was still going on – 2. On the 9th July 1916 he was taking his gun from SCOTS REDOUBT in the direction of the TRIANGLE when nearing the latter place the trench was very heavily shelled wounding one of his team – He sent the remainder of his team on to Lt Smith while he bandaged Pte Hall and then commenced to carry Pte Hall to a dressing station – Another shell partially buried them Cpl Hulett managed to extricate both	

Army Form C. 2118.

21.

WAR DIARY
or
INTELLIGENCE SUMMARY.
(Erase heading not required.)

Instructions regarding War Diaries and Intelligence Summaries are contained in F.S. Regs., Part II. and the Staff Manual respectively. Title pages will be prepared in manuscript.

Place	Date	Hour	Summary of Events and Information	Remarks and references to Appendices
			himself and the man and carried him across the open to the dressing station returning to his gun immediately – Cpl Hulett was slightly wounded himself. 5466 Pte G. RICH on the 7th July 1916 was the No 1 of a gun which was pushed forward in advance of our infantry from BIRCH WOOD to PEAKE WOOD. After the attack the gun was ordered to be withdrawn to BIRCH WOOD and was carried back though a very intense shell fire – The man carrying the tripod was wounded and had to leave it – As soon as Pte Rich had got his gun back to BIRCH WOOD without any hesitation he returned nearly as far as PEAKE WOOD to fetch the tripod although the shelling was still intense. (5466 Pte G. RICH awarded the Military Medal Authority III Corps Memo. No C.R. 3/505/A/16 dated 18-7-16.)	WA WA WA
ALBERT	11-7-16		The Company having been relieved moved from BECOURT WOOD to billets in ALBERT on the night 10-11 – During the period 11th-12th the Company spent the time in cleaning themselves as well as the limbers, harness and guns – The Company bathed on the 12 inst.	WA

T.J.134. Wt. W708-776. 50C000. 4/15. Sir J. C. & S.

Army Form 2118.

WAR DIARY
or
INTELLIGENCE SUMMARY.
(Erase heading not required.)

Instructions regarding War Diaries and Intelligence Summaries are contained in F. S. Regs., Part II. and the Staff Manual respectively. Title pages will be prepared in manuscript.

22

Place	Date	Hour	Summary of Events and Information	Remarks and references to Appendices
ALBERT	13-14 July		Company paraded under section Officers arrangements -	WH
BECOURT WOOD	15-7-16		Company moved up to BECOURT WOOD in reserve to 3rd Division who were attacking POZIERES - Left billets at ALBERT 9AM and arrived at BECOURT WOOD about 9.30AM. No guns sent up during day -	WH
"	16-7-16		Received instructions from Brigade to relieve 112 Machine Gun Company in the trenches - Relief started 2PM and completed by 5PM - On the morning of the 16th a reconnaissance of the positions was made by the O.C and Section Officers	
TRENCHES	17-7-16		RIGHT SECTOR - (4 guns No.1 Section under 2Lt J.A.DOMMETT) - The position of the guns as handed over to his section were as follows - 2 guns mounted on the N.E corner of BAILIFF WOOD - 2 guns in reserve in dug outs in BAILIFF WOOD - After a further reconnaissance it appeared necessary to push the guns forward and the following positions were taken up - 1 gun was placed about 100 yards N. of chalk pit the team digging well in - This gun commanded the road running into POZIERES - 1 gun was placed on the top of a Bluff and had a fine commanding position, but by digging into the side of the Bluff shelter and concealment was	

Army Form C. 2118.

23

WAR DIARY
or
INTELLIGENCE SUMMARY.
(Erase heading not required.)

Place	Date	Hour	Summary of Events and Information	Remarks and references to Appendices
			obtained from most of the enemies shell fire coming from the N.E. 1 gun was placed in position so that it could command our left flank. 1 gun was placed on our forward trench and firing almost due EAST enfiladed the whole of our front in case of a counter attack	
			LEFT SECTOR - (4 guns No 4 Section Lt WARWICK) Took over the 4 guns in support at BAILIFF WOOD from 112 Coy Machine Gun Corps - Received instructions that the Brigade would attack POZIERES - No 4 Section in support pushed their guns forward into the front system. No 3 Section (4 guns) moving up into support at BAILIFF WOOD No 2 Section (4 guns) remained in reserve at Brigade Headquarters.	W.A.
			Report by 2 Lt J.A.DOMMETT on the attack made at 8 P.M. by the Brigade on the enemies trench before POZIERES'. Accompanying Corpl Benn to the gun on the Bluff the proceedings were closely watched and it was hoped that a view of some of the enemys machine Guns might be obtained if placed on his parapet during the attack and so engaged - No enemy movement was seen at all the smoke from the enemys barrage being very dense. The impression was received that the enemys machine guns	

Army Form C. 2118.

WAR DIARY
or
INTELLIGENCE SUMMARY.
(Erase heading not required.)

24

Place	Date	Hour	Summary of Events and Information	Remarks and references to Appendices
TRENCHES	18-7-16		which held up the attack were on the left of the position — During the attack although some rounds were fired into the village yet no target presented itself and little could be done to assist the attacking infantry and this was the state of affairs from a Machine Gunners point of view during the whole stay of the Section in the trenches — Our preliminary bombardment gave the enemy ample warning and he fired red rockets into the air 30.4 minutes before 8 P.M. The attack on the night of the 17th did not develope consequently defensive positions were taken up. No 3 Section withdrew from support in BAILIFF WOOD to reserve in BECOURT WOOD. Thus the location of the guns were as follows:- 6 guns in front system, 2 guns in support at BAILIFF WOOD. The remaining 8 guns in reserve at BECOURT WOOD ready to move at 10 minutes notice —	W.H. W.H.
	19-7-16		Nothing of importance happened — The enemys artillery was very active Company relieved by the 3rd Australian Machine Gun Company — Relief commenced about 9 P.M and was completed by the early hours of the 20th	W.H
ALBERT	20-7-16		Company marched from ALBERT to FRANVILLERS arriving about 2 P.M Company billeted —	

WAR DIARY or **INTELLIGENCE SUMMARY.**
(Erase heading not required.)

Army Form 2118.

25

Place	Date	Hour	Summary of Events and Information	Remarks and references to Appendices
FRANVILLERS	21-7-16 to		During this period the Company remained in billets at FRANVILLERS. During which period the Company spent a great deal of time in cleaning Limbers	WH
	26-7-16		and also the limbers and contents. Short route marches after tea.	
TRENCHES	26-7-16		Received instructions from Brigade to relieve No 3 Machine Gun Company in the trenches at CONTALMAISON. Left FRANVILLERS 9 A.M. and marched to ALBERT. The Company halted just outside ALBERT for dinners. The O.C. Company and Section Officers went on ahead of the Company to reconnoitre the positions of the guns to be taken over. Relief started at 5.30 P.M. and was completed by 9 P.M. Distribution of guns as follows:- No 2 Section (4 guns) in front system, No 3 Section (4 guns) and Head Quarters in support at CONTALMAISON and No 1 and 4 Sections (8 guns) in reserve at BECOURT WOOD ready to move at 10 minutes notice.	WH
	28-7-16		Company relieved from trenches by 69 Machine Gun Company. Relief completed by 7 P.M. The Company went back to billets in ALBERT in reserve.	
ALBERT	29-7-16 to 31-7-16		During this period short route marches carried out. The moral of all ranks is excellent.	WH

H. Hanson Lt
O.C. No 8 Coy. MACHINE GUN CORPS

68th Brigade.
23rd Division.

68th BRIGADE

MACHINE GUN COMPANY

AUGUST 1 9 1 6

VOL 6
Army Form C. 2118.
26

WAR DIARY
or
INTELLIGENCE SUMMARY.
(Erase heading not required.)

Place	Date	Hour	Summary of Events and Information	Remarks and references to Appendices
	1916.			
	29 July		5521 Corpl F.W.G. Hulett awarded Military Medal (Authority III Corps Memo. No. CR3/505 A4/16 dated 26.7.1916 -	WA
TRENCHES	1 Aug		The Company relieved 69 Coy Machine Gun Corps in front system, 2 guns in close support, 4 guns in support at CONTALMAISON and 4 guns in reserve at BECOURT WOOD	WA
"	3 Aug to 5 Aug		Disposition of guns was varied as follows:- Front system 6 - 2 fired on left of objective 2 on the right and 2 on SWITCH - CONTALMAISON 4 guns firing indirect fire on railway and enemy communication trenches - Support at CONTALMAISON 6 guns - 2 in position in front of village and 4 in cellars - At 9.16 P.M. on the 4th 10 guns fired for 5 minutes and at intervals afterwards until it was known that operations were over - The left gun was limited to six its fire by the Anzacs who were fighting on our left - It however was able to pick out on target and secured a few casualties, after that the Anzacs became so mixed up with such of the enemy as could be seen that all we could do was to traverse the enemy parapet - The guns on the right could not see any enemy but traversed the parapet -	WA

Army Form C. 2118.

27

WAR DIARY
or
INTELLIGENCE SUMMARY.
(Erase heading not required.)

Place	Date	Hour	Summary of Events and Information	Remarks and references to Appendices
	1916.			
TRENCHES	3-5 Aug.		The four guns doing indirect fire continued to fire all through the night at enemy communications to give assistance to Anzacs giving a final burst at 5.30 A.M. 5th at which time enemy activity appeared to die down somewhat – On the 5 inst at 11AM and again several times between 2-3 PM small bodies of enemy were observed coming from direction of MARTINPUICH through a cornfield in direction of SWITCH TRENCH. Fire was opened from LANCS. TRENCH. Some Artillery Officers observing for us. We fired some 1000 rounds – The observing officers reported about 25 enemy casualties –	WA
	5 Aug.		Company relieved from trenches by 69 Machine Gun Company – Billeted for night in ALBERT.	WA
ALBERT	6 Aug.		During the day the Company spent most of the time cleaning themselves. About 6 P.M. the Company moved from ALBERT into bivouac under the railway at the western entrance to ALBERT.	WA
	7 Aug.		The Company spent the time cleaning limbers and repacking them	WA
	8 Aug.		The Company moved from under the railway at the western entrance to ALBERT to billets at BEHENCOURT about a 3 hours march.	WA

WAR DIARY or INTELLIGENCE SUMMARY

Army Form C. 2118.

28

Place	Date	Hour	Summary of Events and Information	Remarks and references to Appendices
	1916			
BEHENCOURT	9 Aug		Training carried out as follows. Gun drill, packing limbers and short route march	
	10 Aug		The transport of the Company (tactical vehicals) water cart, cooks cart &c joined the Brigade transport. The Brigade transport under the O.C. 68 Coy Machine Gun Corps moved to POULAINVILLE and billeted for night moving on in the early hours of the morning to new Divison Area.	WA
	11 Aug		The Company marched from BEHENCOURT to FRECHINCOURT and entrained for LONGPRE detraining at LONGPRE about 10.30 P.M. then marched to GORENFLOS and joined the transport — billeted for night at GORENFLOS	
GORENFLOS	12 Aug		The Company complete left GORENFLOS for LONGPRE STATION and entrained about 3 P.M. Left LONGPRE STATION at 6.21 P.M. for BAILLEUL arriving there about 4 A.M. in the morning — Detrained at BAILLEUL and marched to THIEUSHOUK arriving about 8.30 A.M.	
	13 Aug			WA
THIEUSHOUK	14 Aug		Training carried out as follows:- Mechanism, gun drill and short route march	WA
	15 Aug		The Company marched from THIEUSHOUK to transport lines of 123 Machine Gun Company at NEIPPE —	WA

Army Form C. 2118.

29

WAR DIARY
or
INTELLIGENCE SUMMARY.
(Erase heading not required.)

Instructions regarding War Diaries and Intelligence Summaries are contained in F. S. Regs., Part II. and the Staff Manual respectively. Title pages will be prepared in manuscript.

No. 123 COMPANY 6-9-16 MACHINE GUN CORPS

Place	Date	Hour	Summary of Events and Information	Remarks and references to Appendices
	1916			
TRENCHES	16 Aug		The Company relieved 123 Machine Gun Company in the Trenches. Disposition of guns were as follows: Front system 6 guns Support 8 guns Reserve 2 guns —	WA
	17 Aug to 23 Aug		During this period there was very little activity. Some of our guns fired at GAPS and enemy's communications but no targets obtained.	WA
"	24 Aug		At 2.30 A.M. hostile working party was fired on - Party dispersed - Re-appeared 3.30 A.M. again dispersed by fire. It is not definitely known if the enemy suffered casualties.	WA
"	25 Aug to 30 Aug		During this period the enemy Machine Guns very active - Some of our guns fired at suspected Machine Gun emplacements, GAPS and enemy's communications.	WA
"	31 Aug		About 7000 rounds fired at enemy's front line and communications in connection with a Gas attack which was carried out - very little enemy MG fire during the Gas attack. The little enemy MG fire during the Gas attack points to one of two things either enemy were not on the alert or gas interfered with the working of the guns - The latter so I think the case as several guns fired a few short bursts and then for a time stopped altogether —	WA

T.J134. Wt. W708—776. 50000. 4/15. Sir J. C. & S.

Army Form C. 2118.

30

Instructions regarding War Diaries and Intelligence Summaries are contained in F. S. Regs., Part II. and the Staff Manual respectively. Title pages will be prepared in manuscript.

INTELLIGENCE SUMMARY

(Erase heading not required.)

Place	Date	Hour	Summary of Events and Information	Remarks and references to Appendices
	1916. 31st Aug		Reliefs carried out every 4 days. Owing to the number of guns (14) in the line it was found difficult to adopt a system by which reliefs could be carried out and so allow other men to have short rests, owing to the shortage of N.C.O.s and men – On the Brigade Commander relinquishing command of the Brigade for other employment he was pleased to write and say how satisfied he had been with the work of the Company –	WH

[signature]
COMDG. No 68 COY. MACHINE GUN CORPS.

Army Form C. 2118.

3/Vol 7

WAR DIARY
or
INTELLIGENCE SUMMARY.
(Erase heading not required.)

Instructions regarding War Diaries and Intelligence Summaries are contained in F. S. Regs., Part II. and the Staff Manual respectively. Title pages will be prepared in manuscript.

No. 5 COMPANY
5·10·16
MACHINE GUN CORPS

Place	Date	Hour	Summary of Events and Information	Remarks and references to Appendices
	September 1916			
TRENCHES	1st & 2nd		Company in trenches - Nothing of note happened -	W.A
BAILLEUL	3rd		Company relieved from trenches by 154th Machine Gun Company - On completion of relief the Company marched from PONT de NIEPPE (Company Transport coming) to 2 Anzacs Camp near BAILLEUL and remained for night under canvas	W.A
	4th		Left BAILLEUL and marched to LE ROUKLOSHILLE and billeted for night	W.A
	5th		The Company (less Transport) entrained at BAILLEUL for new area detraining at ST OMER and marched to billets at WESTROVE. The transport left by road and marched about 12 miles and then rested for the night - Moved again in the early hours on the morning of the 6th and joined the Company at WESTROVE arriving about 2 o'clock in the afternoon -	W.A
WESTROVE	6th		During this period the following training carried out: - Mechanism (various stages), Physical Drill, Handling of Arms and saluting, Gun Drill, Special instruction in Aircraftmanship, Drivers special instruction in Mechanism and Belt filling, Revolver shooting &c.	
	7th			
	8th			
	9th			W.A
	10th		Left billets at WESTROVE at 1.30 A.M. and marched to AUDRIQUE arriving 4 A.M. Entrained at AUDRIQUE STATION and left at 7.39 a.m. arrived	

Army Form C. 2118.

WAR DIARY
or
INTELLIGENCE SUMMARY.
(Erase heading not required.)

Instructions regarding War Diaries and Intelligence Summaries are contained in F. S. Regs., Part II. and the Staff Manual respectively. Title pages will be prepared in manuscript.

32

Place	Date	Hour	Summary of Events and Information	Remarks and references to Appendices
	September 1916			
MOLLIENS	10th		LONGEAU STATION 3 p.m. detrained and marched to billets at MOLLIENS arriving 7.30 p.m.	WA
	12th		Left MOLLIENS and marched with Brigade to MILLENCOURT. Passed Brigade Starting point 9 A.M. arrived in billets 2 p.m.	WA
MILLENCOURT	13th		The day spent in cleaning of limbers, guns &c. Weather condition unfavourable showers during day.	WA
	14th		The Brigade in Army Reserve. The Company carried on training as follows: Mechanism, Gun Drill, Physical Training. Football match in afternoon against Trench M. Battery.	WA
BECOURT WOOD	15th		Moved from billets at MILLENCOURT into bivouac at BECOURT WOOD	WA
	16th		The Company worked as follows: Cleaning of limbers, guns &c. Improvement of dug outs &c. Football Matches.	WA
	17th		Football Matches	WA
	18th		Moved from BECOURT WOOD to CONTALMAISON in support to the 69th Brigade	WA
CONTALMAISON	19th		Remained in support to 69th Brigade. The Company spent the time as follows	
	20th		Improvement and repairing roads, Building, repairing and draining of	
	21st		dug outs, shelters &c.	WA

WAR DIARY
or
INTELLIGENCE SUMMARY.

Army Form C. 2118.

Place	Date	Hour	Summary of Events and Information	Remarks and references to Appendices
	September 1916			
CONTALMAISON	22nd		Moved from CONTALMAISON relieving 69th Brigade in front system of trenches	W.A.
TRENCHES	23rd		Distribution of guns. Front system 8 guns. Support 8 guns. The ground in front of infantry position reconnoitred with a view of advance. An emplacement was dug in MARTIN'S trench which was also repaired and sandbagged	W.A.
	23rd 24th		Guns were in readiness to assist in the event of counter attacks when the 11 N.F. attacked in the afternoon but were not used. An open emplacement was dug in PRUE trenches. LIEUT. J.S. GOODING wounded whilst reconnoitring for a position for a machine gun in the trench captured by the 11th Northumberland Fus. During this operation the following casualties occured. 1 O.R. killed. 1 O.R. wounded. 1 O.R. accidentally wounded. 2 O.R. wounded at duty	W.A.
	25th		Enemy artillery very active during the night. During the night we fired a number of rounds at enemy's communications	W.A.
	26th		The Company relieved by 70 Machine Gun Company. After which the Company moved back into Divisional reserve	W.A.
	27th		During the day the Company was medical inspected after which sections cleaned and repair lorries &c	W.A.

Army Form C. 2118.

34

WAR DIARY
or
INTELLIGENCE SUMMARY.
(Erase heading not required.)

Place	Date	Hour	Summary of Events and Information	Remarks and references to Appendices
	September 1916.			
	28th		While the Company was in reserve training was carried on as follows:—	
	29th		mechanism, Gun drill, Physical Training, Short route marches also a great deal of time was spent improving transport lines &c	W.A.
	30th		The morale of all ranks in the Company continues to be excellent in spite of the many hardships endured during the inclement weather	W.A.

Wace Major
Comdg. No. 26 Coy. Machine Gun Corps.

WAR DIARY or INTELLIGENCE SUMMARY

Army Form C. 2118.

Vol 8

35

Place	Date	Hour	Summary of Events and Information	Remarks and references to Appendices
	October 1916			
	1		In reserve	R/M
CONTALMAISON	2		Company moved up into support at CONTALMAISON relieving No 69 Company Machine Gun Corps	R/M
Before LE SARS	3		Company relieved No 149 Company Machine Gun Corps in front line trenches before LE SARS. Dispositions: eight guns in front system — four in support — four in reserve. Weather wet	R/M R/M
	4		In trenches. Enemy artillery active	
	5		Weather continued bad causing some sickness. Enemy artillery active especially against SPENCE TRENCH and its vicinity which were shelled off & on all day. No targets	R/M
	6		Enemy artillery activity continued. Front system reconnoitred with a view to cooperating in offensive action on the next day. Under cover of darkness a gun was pushed well forward on right of village.	R/M
	7	1.45pm	Intense bombardment of LE SARS prior to infantry attack. Intense infantry attack which followed had two objectives (1) the sunken	

R.M. McMurr Lt M.G. Major
Comdg. No 65 Coy. MACHINE GUN CORPS

WAR DIARY
or
INTELLIGENCE SUMMARY.
(Erase heading not required.)

Army Form C. 2118.

36

road to the right (SOUTH) of LE SARS. (2) the enemy trench EAST of the village. Machine Guns in front of system cooperated in attack which was successful. Right flank however was endangered by failure of troops of division on our right to get forward. Three guns of this company covered this exposed flank and the situation not - two being pushed well forward. These two guns are in particular the one already pushed forward the night before got good targets at close range and did considerable execution holding up the enemy who were endeavouring to counterattack from the right. After the second objective had been obtained two of support guns were pushed up into our original front line and two guns from our originals were pushed up into the new line beyond (EAST) of LE SARS according the Infantry to this. These positions were maintained - dispositions being - two guns in front line beyond (EAST) of LE SARS, three guns protecting sunken road and right flank, five guns in close support in line from what we had attacked, two guns in support and four in reserve.

[signed] L.H. Major
COMDG. NO. 6 COY. MACHINE GUN CORPS

[stamp: No. 6 COMPANY 18 NOV 1916 MACHINE GUN CORPS]

WAR DIARY
or
INTELLIGENCE SUMMARY.
(Erase heading not required.)

Army Form C. 2118.

37

Place	Date	Hour	Summary of Events and Information	Remarks and references to Appendices
	8		Position at tannis wood, relieved at night when company was relieved by No 6 Coy 14th Company Machine Gun Corps. Enemy artillery very active all day. Fair amount of enemy gunfire on several occasions during day on parties of enemy moving about and working in front of our positions.	R/w
	9		Bivouacked at BECOURT WOOD	A/w
	10		Cleaning and repacking limbers	R/w
	11		Entrained at ALBERT	R/w
	12		Detrained at LONGPRÉ and marched to ST. RIQUIER	R/w
	13th		Entrained at ST. RIQUIER	R/w
	15		Detrained at PROVEN and marched to ERIE CAMP	R/w
	16		At ERIE CAMP refitting	R/w
	17	10pm	Relieved from No 6 and No 7 Australian M.G. Companies in YPRES salient HOOGE - VINGE STREET sector. Guns - 10 in second line + in support. I am reserve + I Ordnance in reserve	R/w
	18		In trenches. A/M enemy shelling at 5pm and 9pm	R/w

Matthews 2/Lt
COMDG. NO 68 COY. MACHINE GUN CORPS

[Stamp: NO 68 COMPANY 8 NOV 1916 MACHINE GUN]

Army Form C. 2118.

36

WAR DIARY
or
INTELLIGENCE SUMMARY.
(Erase heading not required.)

Instructions regarding War Diaries and Intelligence Summaries are contained in F. S. Regs, Part II. and the Staff Manual respectively. Title pages will be prepared in manuscript.

Place	Date	Hour	Summary of Events and Information	Remarks and references to Appendices
	19		Quiet. 2250 rounds fired during night at enemy communications	O/c
	20		Some intermittent shelling during day. Otherwise quiet. 1000 rounds fired at enemy's communications during night	R/W
	21		Quiet. 2300 rounds fired at enemy communications during night	R/W
	22		Gas alarm heard from right 7 p.m. No gas over. Quiet. 500 rounds fired during night at enemy communications	O/W
	23		Relieved by 169 Company at night. Entrained at YPRES, detrained and went into billets at POPERINGHE.	R/W
	24		At POPERINGHE cleaning guns ammunition etc	R/W
	25		At POPERINGHE - training	R/W
	26		At POPERINGHE - training	R/W
	27		At POPERINGHE - Inspected by G.O.C II Army	R/W
	28		At POPERINGHE - training	R/W
	29	8.30pm	Relieved 70 Company Machine Gun Corps in VINCE STREET - ARMAGH WOOD sectors. Some hostile M.G. fire and sniping during night -	R/W

R. William 2/Lt.
COMDG. NO. 65 COY. MACHINE GUN CORP.

Army Form C. 2118.

WAR DIARY
or
INTELLIGENCE SUMMARY.
(Erase heading not required.)

Place	Date	Hour	Summary of Events and Information	Remarks and references to Appendices
				34
	30.		otherwise quiet. Guns – 8 enfront system – 4 outpost 4 reserve	Rpr Rpr Rpr Rpr
	31.		Quiet Quiet	

NO. X COMPANY
3 NOV 1916
MACHINE GUN CORPS

WAR DIARY or INTELLIGENCE SUMMARY

Army Form C. 2118.

November 40

Place	Date	Hour	Summary of Events and Information	Remarks and references to Appendices
	1916 November			
	1.		In trenches. Quiet. Weather wet. Nothing of importance to report	R/W
	2.		Quiet	R/W
	3.		Quiet. Continuance of wet weather necessitated continual repairing	R/W
	4.		Some artillery activity during afternoon. Otherwise quiet	R/W
	5.		Quiet. Nothing to report	
	6.		One of support guns pushed forward into front system leaving Four reserve guns in support. Four reserve guns moved up to YPRES.	R/W
	7.		Some intermittent shelling during day. Otherwise quiet.	R/W
	8.		Quiet.	R/W
	9.	10.15 p.m	Trench mortar and artillery activity during afternoon. Nightquar Relieved by No.69 Company Machine Gun Corps. Went	R/W R/W
	10.		into camp and billets near VLAMERTINGHE. Cleaning and refitting	R/W R/W
	11.		Training. Five Officers and 32 O.R. inoculated TAB.	R/W
	12.		Training and improving camp. 2 Officers and 41 O.R. inoculated TAB.	R/W
	13.		Training. Fitting respirators and gas drill	R/W

P. Wallace Lieut
O.C. No.V Co. MACHINE GUN CORP.

Army Form C. 2118.

WAR DIARY
or
INTELLIGENCE SUMMARY.
(Erase heading not required.)

Instructions regarding War Diaries and Intelligence Summaries are contained in F. S. Regs., Part II. and the Staff Manual respectively. Title pages will be prepared in manuscript.

41.

Place	Date	Hour	Summary of Events and Information	Remarks and references to Appendices
	1916 November			
	13		44 O.R. inoculated T.A.B.	RJM
	14		Training.	RJM
	15	11 a.m.	Inspected by G.O.C. Xth Corps and G.O.C. 68th Brigade	RJM
		10 p.m.	Relieved N° 70 Company Machine Gun Corps in trenches - HOOGE - VINCE STREET sector. Dispositions - 9 guns front system, 3 in support, 4 in reserve	
	16		In trenches. Quiet.	RJM
	17		Day quiet. Trench mortars of Brigade on immediate left bombarded enemy trenches from 11 to 11.30 p.m. Night on our front quiet.	RJM
	18		Quiet	RJM
	19		Enemy trench mortars and artillery active during afternoon.	RJM
	20		Night - quiet with some enemy M.G. fire. Enemy shelled ZILLEBEKE during afternoon. YEOMANRY POST swept by enemy M.G. at intervals during night.	RJM
	21		Quiet. YEOMANRY POST again swept by M.G. 2500 rounds fired (indirect) on enemy supports and communications	RJM

RJMillar Lieut
COMDG. No. 68

Army Form C. 2118.

WAR DIARY
or
INTELLIGENCE SUMMARY.
(Erase heading not required.)

Instructions regarding War Diaries and Intelligence Summaries are contained in F. S. Regs., Part II. and the Staff Manual respectively. Title pages will be prepared in manuscript.

4-2

Place	Date	Hour	Summary of Events and Information	Remarks and references to Appendices
	1916 November			
	22		Quiet 1500 rounds fired at enemy communications.	Rpt.
	23		WELLINGTON CRESCENT shelled. Enemy M.Gs active during night.	Rpt.
	24.		1000 rounds fired on enemy communications. Artillery active during afternoon. Night quiet.	Rpt. Rpt.
	25.		Quiet.	Rpt.
	26		Some enemy artillery activity during day. 1000 rounds fired during night at enemy communications	Rpt.
	27		Enemy artillery active during afternoon. 500 rounds fired at enemy dumps in CHATEAU WOOD HOOGE.	Rpt.
	28		Quiet. Relieved by No 70 Company Machine Gun Corps and went into camp at CAMP ERIE.	Rpt.
	29.		Cleaning guns ammunition equipment &c. Baths for men	Rpt. Rpt.
	30		Training. Constructing transport lines	Rpt.

RMcClure Lieut
COMDG. No 66 COY MACHINE GUN CORPS

Army Form C. 2118.

40

WAR DIARY
or
INTELLIGENCE SUMMARY.
(Erase heading not required.)

Place	Date	Hour	Summary of Events and Information	Remarks and references to Appendices
	1916 November			
	1.		In trenches. Weather wet. Nothing of importance to report	Qur.
	2.		Quiet	R/W
	3.		Quiet. Continuance of wet weather necessitated considerable repairing	R/W
	4.		Some artillery activity during afternoon. Otherwise quiet	R/W
	5.		Quiet. Nothing to report	
	6.		One of support guns firing indirect frontal ands front system harvey	R/W
			Three guns in support. Four reserve guns moved up to YPRES.	R/W
			Some intermittent shelling during day. Otherwise quiet	R/W
	7.		Quiet	R/W
	8.		Trench mortar and artillery activity during afternoon. Night quiet	R/W
	9.	10.15	Relieved by No. 69 Company Machine Gun Corps. Went	R/W
	10.		into camp on billets near VLAMERTINGHE. Bathing and refitting	R/W
	11.		Training. Five officers and 32 O.R. inoculated TAB.	R/W
	12.		Training and inspection camp. 2 Officers and 40 O.R. inoculated TAB	R/W
	13.		Training. Fitting respirators and gas drill. 1 Officer and	R/W

No. 68 COMPANY MACHINE GUN

O.C. No. 68 Coy MACHINE GUN CORPS.

Army Form C. 2118.

4-1.

WAR DIARY
or
INTELLIGENCE SUMMARY.
(Erase heading not required.)

Place	Date	Hour	Summary of Events and Information	Remarks and references to Appendices
	1916 November			
	13		44 O.R. nominated T.A.B	R/W
	14		Training	R/W
	15	11 a.m.	Inspected by G.O.C. X th Corps and G.O.C. 63rd Brigade	R/W
		10 p.m.	Relieved No 70 Company Machine Gun Corps in trenches - HOOGE - VINCE STREET sector. Dispositions - 9 guns front system, 3 in support H in reserve	R/W
	16		In trenches. Quiet.	R/W R/W
	17		Day quiet. Trench mortars active on immediate left bombarded enemy trenches from 11 to 11.30 p.m. Night on our front quiet.	R/W R/W
	18		Quiet	R/W
	19		Enemy trench mortars and artillery active during afternoon. Nng M.G. - quiet with some enemy M.G. fire	R/W
	20		Enemy shelled ZILLEBEKE during afternoon. YEOMANRY POST swept by enemy M.G. at intervals every night 2500	R/W
	21		Quiet. YEOMANRY POST again swept by M.G. rounds fired (machine) on enemy support and communications	R/W

WAR DIARY
or
INTELLIGENCE SUMMARY.
(Erase heading not required.)

Army Form C. 2118.

42

Instructions regarding War Diaries and Intelligence Summaries are contained in F.S. Regs., Part II. and the Staff Manual respectively. Title pages will be prepared in manuscript.

Place	Date	Hour	Summary of Events and Information	Remarks and references to Appendices
1916 November	22		Quiet. 1500 rounds fired at enemy communications.	R.H.
	23		WELLINGTON CRESCENT shelled. Enemy M.Gs active during night.	R.H.
	24		1500 rounds fired on enemy communications. Artillery active during afternoon. Night quiet.	R.H.
	25		Quiet.	R.H.
	26		Some enemy artillery activity during day. 1000 rounds fired during night on enemy communications.	R.H.
	27		Enemy artillery active during afternoon. 500 rounds fired at enemy dumps in CHATEAU WOOD RIDGE.	R.H.
	28		Relieved by No 70 Company Machine Gun Corps and went into camp at CAMP ERIE.	R.H.
	29		Cleaning guns, ammunition, equipment etc. Baths for men.	R.H.
	30		Training. Constructing transport lines.	R.H.

R. Matthews Lieut
68 Machine Gun Corps

T2134. Wt. W708—776. 500000. 4/15. Sir J. C. & S.

WAR DIARY
or
INTELLIGENCE SUMMARY.

(Erase heading not required.) No 68 Company Machine Gun Corps

Army Form C. 2118.

Vol 70 pt 2

Place	Date	Hour	Summary of Events and Information	Remarks and references to Appendices
	1916 December			
ERIE CAMP	1		Training constructing transport lines and improving camp	RM
	2		Training construction of transport lines and improving camp	RM
	3		Training constructing transport lines and improving camp	RM
	4		Training constructing transport lines and improving camp	RM
	5		Training constructing transport lines and improving camp	RM
TRENCHES [YPRES]	6	9.30 p.m.	Relieved No 70 Company Machine Gun Corps in trenches. Dispositions - 11 guns in forward system; 5 in support group.	RM
	7		VINE ST. - ARMAGH WOOD sector. RUDKIN HOUSE shelled at intervals 2-4 p.m. Night quiet.	RM
	8		Trench mortars and artillery active during afternoon	RM
			RUDKIN HOUSE again shelled 2-4 pm	RM
	9		Nothing to report	RM
	10		Nothing to report	RM
	11		Nothing to report	RM
	12		Nothing to report	RM
	13		Intermittent artillery activity during day. SR torpedo fired	RM

SM Summer Capt

WAR DIARY
or
INTELLIGENCE SUMMARY.
(Erase heading not required.)

Army Form C. 2118.

Place	Date	Hour	Summary of Events and Information	Remarks and references to Appendices
	13		(which at M.41 I.36 a.66 to KLEIN ZILLEBEKE = Intermittent artillery activity during day	Rpu. Rpu.
	14		Some artillery activity during afternoon. Several shells fell near RUDKIN HOUSE about 4 p.m.	Rpu.
	15		Enemy artillery and trench mortars very active particularly from 7 to 10 a.m. and 4 to 6 p.m. OBSERVATORY RIDGE heavily shelled.	Rpu.
	16		Some enemy artillery activity 1 to 1.30 p.m. but otherwise generally quiet.	Rpu.
	17		Quiet.	Rpu.
	18		Quiet. Warned by Brigade Camp that would be blown on HILL 60 at 2 a.m. tomorrow which might detonate large mine. HALIFAX ST. gun (and an enemy's attempts behind HILL 60) ordered to be in readiness to open fire immediately of situation demanded. Other guns held in readiness for any necessary action.	Rpu.

Maj. Simmins Capt.
COMDG. No.6 C.O.Y. MACHINE GUN CORPS

WAR DIARY or INTELLIGENCE SUMMARY.

Army Form C. 2118.

(Erase heading not required.)

Place	Date	Hour	Summary of Events and Information	Remarks and references to Appendices
	1916 December			
	19 Dec		Barrage only completed on HILL 60. No apparent action followed.	
			Day quiet. Night quiet.	9pm
	20		Enemy artillery active during morning OBSERVATORY RIDGE and neighbourhood shelled.	9pm.
	21		Enemy artillery active at intervals during whole day. Enemy emplacement at REDAN damaged but repaired. Alternative emplacement at REDAN damaged but repaired.	9pm
	22		Some intermittent enemy artillery activity during day. Relieved by 69 Company Machine Gun Corps relief being superior by vigorous enemy artillery activity at about 6 pm when ZILLEBEKE was shelled. Relief complete 9.15pm. Marched to huts	9pm 9pm
	= Aug 23	at ERIE CAMP	Resting	9pm
	24		Resting and rearranged constructing horse lines	9pm
	25		Resting and constructing horse lines	9pm
	26		Resting and constructing horse lines	9pm

E. M. Simmons Capt.

WAR DIARY
or
INTELLIGENCE SUMMARY.
(Erase heading not required.)

Army Form C. 2118.

Place	Date	Hour	Summary of Events and Information	Remarks and references to Appendices
	1916 December			
	27		Training and constructing horse lines	R/F/M
	28		Training and constructing horse lines	R/M
	29		Training and constructing horse lines	Y/D
Jundis γmes	30	9.40	Relieved No 70 Coy Machine Gun Corps in the trenches	
			MENIN ROAD - VINCE ST - Exclusive Disposition 9 guns in	
			fire system and 1 in support.	
	31		Enemy artillery shelled in vicinity of Bty HQ and support lines	
			of the trenches during mid day	
	1917 Jan			
	1		Artillery active at mid night. LEINSTER ST - OXFORD ST	
			Shelled at mid day.	

Sy Summer Capt.
O.C. 65 COY. MACHINE GUN CORPS

Confidential War Diary

of No 68 Company

Machine Gun Corps

from 1st January 1917

to 1st February 1917

Army Form C. 2118.

WAR DIARY
or
INTELLIGENCE SUMMARY.
(Erase heading not required.)

46

Place	Date	Hour	Summary of Events and Information	Remarks and references to Appendices
TRENCHES YPRES.	1917 Jan 1.		Nothing to report	91A
	2.		1000 rounds fired on HOOGE	91D
	3.		Nothing to report	91D
	4.		Nothing to report	91D
	5.		Nothing to report	91D
	6.		500 rounds fired on Stirling Bastle	91D
	7.		C.S.M. n Orderly Room Sergeant killed by shell fire at Coy H.Qrs	91D
	8.		1000 rounds fired on STIRLING CASTLE	91D
	9.		Nothing to report	91D
	10.		500 rounds fired on STIRLING CASTLE	91D
	11.		500 rounds fired on STIRLING CASTLE	91D
	12.		Nothing to report	91D

J Dommett Lt-
for O.C. 68 Bug. C

WAR DIARY
or
INTELLIGENCE SUMMARY.

Army Form C. 2118.

47

Place	Date	Hour	Summary of Events and Information	Remarks and references to Appendices
TRENCHES	Jan 13.		The S.O.S signal was sent up during the night on the Brigade on the left. The two left guns in our line opened fire on their barrage lines firing about 1000 rounds each.	J.D.
YPRES.	14.		800 rounds were fired on STIRLING CASTLE	J.D.
	15.		Quiet. Relieved by 69th Coy Machine Gun Corps, and went into camp at EYRIE CAMP.	J.D.
EYRIE CAMP	16.		Refitting and clothing	J.D.
	17.		Training and constructing horse lines	J.D.
	18.		Training and constructing horse lines	J.D.
	19.		Training and constructing horse lines	J.D.
	20.		Training and constructing horse lines	J.D.
	21.		Working party of 70 men and 1 Officer found for Brigade	J.D.
	22.		Training	J.D.
	23.		Preparing for line	J.D.

J. Sommer Lt
for O.C. 68. M.G. C.

Army Form C. 2118.

WAR DIARY
or
INTELLIGENCE SUMMARY.
(Erase heading not required.)

4.8.

Place	Date	Hour	Summary of Events and Information	Remarks and references to Appendices
TRENCHES YPRES	Jan 24th		Relieved No 70 Bay. Machine gun Corps in the Trenches VINCE ST ARMAGH WOOD sector. Disposition of guns being 11 in the front system and 5 in support	9th D
	25.		Noticeable menace in aerial and artillery activity	9th D
	26.		Nothing to report	9th D
	27.		Remarked artillery activity	9th D
	28.		Nothing to report	9th D
	29.		Artillery active	9th D
	30.		Hard Frost.	9th D
	31.		Hard Frost	9th D

J.K. Dommett Lt.
for O.C. 60 M.G. C.

Confidential

War Diary

of

No. 68 Company

Machine Gun Corps

from 1st February 1917.
to 1st March, 1917.

Vol 2

Army Form C. 2118.

WAR DIARY
or
INTELLIGENCE SUMMARY.

(Erase heading not required.)

49

Place	Date	Hour	Summary of Events and Information	Remarks and references to Appendices
In the Trenches YPRES	1917 Oct 1.		The S.O.S was observed on the left. There was a heavy local bombardment	JAD
	2.		Nothing to report	JAD
	3.		Nothing to report	JAD
	4.		Nothing to report	
	5.		Nothing to report	
	6.		Nothing to report	
	7.		The guns mounted at night in the REDAN ~ RUDKIN HOUSE were slightly damaged by shell fire. They were replaced by guns from the support group, and repairs effected the same day by the Company Artificer.	
	8.		Relieved by 69 Coy, and returned to Billets in Ypres Camp.	
Ypres Camp	9.		Refitting and Baths	
	10.			
	11.			
	12.		Training carried out in accordance with scheme submitted to Brigade	
	13.			
	14.			
	15.			

J.A. Sommers Lieut for
O.C.
Comdg. No. 68 Co. Machine Gun Corps.

WAR DIARY
or
INTELLIGENCE SUMMARY
(Erase heading not required.)

Army Form C. 2118.

5 – 0

Place	Date	Hour	Summary of Events and Information	Remarks and references to Appendices
Trenches YPRES	1917 Feb 16		Relieved 69th Coy in the MENIN ROAD – VINCE STREET SECTOR.	
	17		Nothing to report	
	18		Nothing to report	
	19		Nothing to report	
	20		Nothing to report	
	21		1500 rounds were fired on STERLING CASTLE	
	22		Nothing to report. The S.O.S. sent up during the night to test rockets was unobserved from any of the gun positions owing to a thick mist.	
	23		Nothing to report	
	24		Nothing to report	
	25		During the night the gun at YEOMANRY POST was moved forward some 200 yards into a new concrete emplacement named THE FORT. An advance party of officers of 117th M.G.B. reconnoitred the line, and attached gun positions unapproachable by day were relieved by gun teams from the 117th M.G.B.	
	26		The relief of the Company was completed by 117th Coy and Company marched to S Camp	

Comdg. No. 63 Co. Machine Gun Corps

Army Form C. 2118.

5/

WAR DIARY
or
INTELLIGENCE SUMMARY.
(Erase heading not required.)

Instructions regarding War Diaries and Intelligence Summaries are contained in F. S. Regs., Part II. and the Staff Manual respectively. Title pages will be prepared in manuscript.

Place	Date	Hour	Summary of Events and Information	Remarks and references to Appendices
Camp S.	1917 Feb 27		Refitting. Billeting party sent forward	
	28		Marched with transport from "S" camp to HERZEELE about 10 miles, and stayed in billets there the night. 2 men fell out during the march	

J.A. Dimmett Lieut for OC.
Comdg. No. 68 Co. Machine Gun Corps

Vol 13

Confidential.

War Diary.

March, 1917.

No. 68 Company
Machine Gun Corps.

Army Form C. 2118.

WAR DIARY
or
INTELLIGENCE SUMMARY.
(Erase heading not required.)

52

Instructions regarding War Diaries and Intelligence Summaries are contained in F. S. Regs., Part II. and the Staff Manual respectively. Title pages will be prepared in manuscript.

Place	Date	Hour	Summary of Events and Information	Remarks and references to Appendices
MERCKEGHEM	1917 Nov 1.		Arrived at MERCKEGHEM at mid-day from HERZEELE the distance being about 15 miles. No one fell out during the march. Billets were taken over.	A.D.
	2.		Cleaning guns and spare parts. Refilling belts.	A.D.
	3.		Elementary drill.	A.D.
	4.		Training	A.D.
	5.		Training	A.D.
	6.		do	A.D.
	7.		do	A.D.
	8.		do	A.D.
	9.		do	A.D.
	10.		Training. Field day with D.M.G.O.	A.D.
	11.		Training	A.D.
	12.		do	A.D.
	13.		do	A.D.
	14.		do	A.D.
	15.		do	A.D.
	16.		do	A.D.
	17.		do	A.D.
	18.		do	A.D.

M Dommett Lieut.

Army Form C. 2118.

WAR DIARY
or
INTELLIGENCE SUMMARY.
(Erase heading not required.)

53

Place	Date 1917	Hour	Summary of Events and Information	Remarks and references to Appendices
MERCKEGHEM	May 19.		Marched with Transport from MERCKEGHEM to HOUTKERQUE, distance about 18 miles. No one fell out during the march. Billets were taken over. Arrived at 3-30 p.m.	JR
"	20.		Marched with Transport from HOUTKERQUE to "Y" Camp, distance 4 to 5 miles.	JR
"Y" Camp	21.		Marched from "Y" Camp to "S" Camp and took over huts and quarters. Arrived at 2 p.m.	JR
"S" Camp	22.		Gun cleaning, inspecting billets, ammunition, etc.	JR
"	23.		Training. Tactical scheme with practice in indirect fire.	JR
"	24.		Mechanism, stoppages, rc. Cleaning guns and belt filling practice.	JR
"	25.		Working Party at 8-30 p.m. under Orderly Officer — 50 O. Ranks. Remainder of Company Cleaning guns, Inspection of kennels & belts.	JR
"	26.		Training. 7.15 p.m. Working Party - 1 Officer & 50 O. Ranks. work - burying cable.	JR
"	27.		One section on 100 yds. Range. Remainder - Route march. 7-15 p.m. Working Party — 1 Officer and 50 O. Ranks. Work - burying cable.	JR
"	28.		Training. Mechanism, stoppages, etc.	JR
"	29.		One section on 30 yds Range. Remainder on Route March and Tactical Exercises.	JR
"	30.		Training.	JR
"	31.		8.0 am. Working party at R.E. Yard, PESELHOEK at A. 21. a. 2.1. 28 O. Ranks. One section on 100 yds. range. 2 sections on inspection parade and work in camp.	JR

J. Sommers Lieut

Confidential.

War Diary

of

No. 68 Coy.

Machine Gun Corps.

From 1st April, 1917 to 30th April, 1917.

Vol 14

Original.

Army Form C. 2118.

WAR DIARY
or
INTELLIGENCE SUMMARY.
(Erase heading not required.)

54

Instructions regarding War Diaries and Intelligence Summaries are contained in F. S. Regs., Part II. and the Staff Manual respectively. Title pages will be prepared in manuscript.

Place	Date	Hour	Summary of Events and Information	Remarks and references to Appendices
Champ. D.	1917 April 1		Training in Reserve.	JRD
"	2		do.	JRD
"	3		do.	JRD
"	4		Move to MERCKEGHEM. Company entrained at BRANDHOEK and detrained at ESQUELBECQ and marched to billets at Merckeghem. Transport moved by road to billets, MERCKEGHEM. Company arrived at 6 pm. Transport arrived at 6-30 p.m.	JRD
MERCKEGHEM	5-11th		Training in Reserve.	JRD
"	12th		Half Company with half transport moved to ABEELE to take over a-aircraft positions. Remaining half company moved to ESQUELBECQ and entrained for ERIE CAMP. Detrained at POPERINGHE and marched to ERIE CAMP arriving at 2-0 pm. Remaining half transport moved by road arriving at ERIE CAMP at 4-0 pm.	JRD
"	13th		Half Company at ABEELE.	JRD
ABEELE	13th		Half Company at ABEELE.	JRD
ERIE CAMP	14th		Half Company left ERIE CAMP at 8-30 pm + entrained to YPRES and took over 8 gun positions in HOOGE SECTOR. Coy. HQ. took over 116 M.G. Coy HQ. at YPRES.	JRD
ABEELE	14th		Half Company at ABEELE.	JRD
In trenches	15th		" " in trenches and half company at ABEELE	JRD

J.P. Sommers Lieut
for O.C. 62 M.G. C.

Army Form C. 2118.

WAR DIARY
or
INTELLIGENCE SUMMARY.
(Erase heading not required.)

55

Place	Date	Hour	Summary of Events and Information	Remarks and references to Appendices
In trenches	1917 April 16th		Half company in trenches. Half company at ABEELE moved to ERIE CAMP and transport by road.	
"	17th		Half Company in trenches. Remaining half company entrained from BRANDHOEK and detrained at YPRES and took over 8 additional gun positions in HOOGE SECTOR.	
"	18th		Company in trenches	
"	19th		Ditto.	
"	20		do	
"	21		do	
"	22		do	One man slightly wounded in hand.	
"	23		do	
"	24		do	
"	25		do	
"	26		do	
"	27		do	
"	28		do	
"	29		do	
"	30		do. No. 58 M.G. Coy commenced to take over at 12 noon and relief of front line positions was still in progress at 12 midnight.	

W Dommett Lieut
for O.C. 68 M.G. C.

Original.

Confidential.

War Diary.

From:- 1st May, 1917.
To:- 31st May, 1917.

No. 68 Coy.
Machine Gun Corps.

3-6-1917.

Army Form C. 2118.

WAR DIARY
or
INTELLIGENCE SUMMARY.
(Erase heading not required.)

54

Place	Date	Hour	Summary of Events and Information	Remarks and references to Appendices
YPRES	1/5/17		Company entrained at YPRES STATION at 1-30 p.m. and detrained at GODEWAERSVELDE STATION at 2-30 a.m. and marched to billets at STEENVOORDE arriving at 3-30 a.m. Transport proceeded by road from ERIE CAMP to Transport Lines near billets at STEENVOORDE arriving at 3-45 a.m.	J.D.
STEENVOORDE	2/5/17 to 8/5/17		Company in training in Training Area at STEENVOORDE.	J.D.
	9/5/17		Company marched with transport from billets at STEENVOORDE to WINNIPEG CAMP arriving at destination at 1-45 p.m. and took over billets. Transport then proceeded to lines at ERIE CAMP.	J.D.
WINNIPEG CAMP	10/5/17		Company training in CAMP.	J.D.
	11/5/17		Company left WINNIPEG CAMP at 9 p.m. and entrained at BRANDHOEK at 9-40 p.m. and detrained at YPRES at 10-15 p.m. Company then marched to trenches and took over gun positions in HILL 60 — HOOGE SECTOR. Company H.Q. taken over at RAILWAY DUGOUTS. Relief complete about 1 a.m. 12/5/17.	J.D.
In the Trenches	12/5/17		Company in trenches.	J.D.

J.Ammett Reut
for O.C. 68th Coy M.G.C.

Army Form C. 2118.

WAR DIARY
or
INTELLIGENCE SUMMARY.
(Erase heading not required.)

55

Place	Date	Hour	Summary of Events and Information	Remarks and references to Appendices
In trenches	13/5/17		Company in trenches.	APD
	14/5/17		"	APD
	15/5/17		One gun damaged and replaced.	APD
	16/5/17		"	APD
	17/5/17		One O.R. killed in action.	APD
	18/5/17		"	APD
	19/5/17		Company relieved by 69th M.G. Coy. + proceeded to Winnipeg Camp Relief completed about 2-30 am	APD
	20/5/17		Company in training.	APD
WINNIPEG CAMP	21/5/17		"	APD
	22/5/17		"	APD
	23/5/17		Company relieved 194 Coy. in Observatory Ridge sector.	APD
In trenches	24/5/17		Relief complete 3-0 am.	APD
	25/5/17		Company in trenches. One mule killed by enemy M.G. fire.	APD
	26/5/17		One mule killed by enemy M.G. fire.	APD
	27/5/17		One O.R. wounded in action.	APD
	28/5/17		One O.R. wounded in action.	APD

J A Dommett Lieut
for O.C. 68 v Coy My. C.

Army Form C. 2118.

56

WAR DIARY
or
INTELLIGENCE SUMMARY.
(Erase heading not required.)

Place	Date	Hour	Summary of Events and Information	Remarks and references to Appendices
In Trenches	29/5/17		Company relieved by 194 Bay. Relief complete 2-30 p.m. Company proceeded to Dominion Lines	9/R
Dominion Lines	30/5/17		Company proceeded to "M" Camp and took over Divisional Distance 2 Kilom	9/R
M Camp	31/5/17		Company in Training. Company in Training	9/R 9/R

J A Dommett Lieut for
O.C. 66th Coy Inf. C.

Original

Confidential

War Diary

of

No 68 Coy. Machine Gun Corps

From 1st June 1917

to 30th June 1917

Army Form C. 2118.

WAR DIARY
or
INTELLIGENCE SUMMARY.
(Erase heading not required.)

Instructions regarding War Diaries and Intelligence Summaries are contained in F. S. Regs., Part II. and the Staff Manual respectively. Title pages will be prepared in manuscript.

Place	Date	Hour	Summary of Events and Information	Remarks and references to Appendices
TRENCHES HILL 60 Sector	June 1		Offensive operations being imminent, and information coming to hand that the Company would be required to put up a barrage with all its guns, work was commenced on making emplacements and dumping ammunition. 32 men from Brigade were attached to assist the Company before & during operations. This work began on the 22nd ult. and was completed this day. Two lines with 16 emplacements at each were required, the first line being for the barrage in front of the first two objectives, and the second line for the final objective. It was estimated that 1,000,000 rounds would be required, which were brought up in limbers at night at the rate of 200,000 a night and dumped as near the position as possible and man handled from there. Three mules were killed in the brakes. Belt filling centres and shelter for gun teams were constructed. Artillery on both sides very active. 10,000 rounds were fired during the night on enemy communications.	[signature] Lieut

A6945 Wt. W14432/M1160 350,000 12/16 D. D. & L. Forms/C./2118/14.

WAR DIARY
or
INTELLIGENCE SUMMARY.
(Erase heading not required.)

Army Form C. 2118.

Place	Date	Hour	Summary of Events and Information	Remarks and references to Appendices
TRENCHES HILL 60 Sector	JUNE 2		Artillery on both sides very active. 10000 rounds were fired during night on enemy communications.	C
	3		Artillery on both sides very active. 2 day rations were dumped near Coy. H.Q. which were constructed near the first rear line of emplacements, with a supply of water. It was decided that the guns would be divided into 2 batteries of 8 guns each, known as I + J batteries respectively, and battery commanders were appointed. Telephone lines were laid from Coy. N.Q. to Battery Commanders H.Q. in the first line, and from Coy. H.Q.s to Brigade H.Q.s. Upon the guns moving forward to the 2nd line of emplacements it was decided that Coy. H.Q. would move to Brigade H.Q. in LARCH WOOD. Telephone lines were not laid from 2nd Coy. H.Q. as it was thought they would be destroyed, the intention being to keep communication by visual Signalling + runners. Map marked "A" attached showing objectives, barrage lines + battery positions. Appendix marked "B" attached giving time table rate of fire etc. 10,000 rounds were fired during the night on enemy communications.	C

Bentley Lieut.

WAR DIARY
or
INTELLIGENCE SUMMARY.

(Erase heading not required.)

Army Form C. 2118.

Place	Date	Hour	Summary of Events and Information	Remarks and references to Appendices
TRENCHES HILL 60 Sector	JUNE 4		for water. 3 petrol cans per gun at each position were dumped for cooling purposes. The Bdy. was now in possession of 60 gun barrels and 2 chronometers received from the D.M.G.O. Battery Commanders fixed their ZERO LINES. Information was received that this was W day calculating from Z or ZERO day. At dark all the guns were withdrawn from the line two sections being placed in MANOR FARM and 2 sections in RAILWAY DUGOUTS. The only relief being of a forward guns by 69 Bdy M.G.C. 10,000 rounds were used for harassing fire from back positions during the night.	R.
	5		Artillery active.	R.
	6	7pm	Information received that ZERO hour was 3:10 a.m. on 7th inst. At dark sections moved to the first rear line of emplacements, 6 guns commencing harrassing fire.	R.

Cowlthy Lieut

WAR DIARY
or
INTELLIGENCE SUMMARY.
(Erase heading not required.)

Army Form C. 2118.

Place	Date	Hour	Summary of Events and Information	Remarks and references to Appendices
TRENCHES HILL 60 Sector	6th	11pm	H.Qs moved to near of 1st Bn. H.Q. 2nd in command taking command. O.C. going to 2nd Bn. H.Qs in LARCH WOOD to take command after the Bn had moved forward to the 2nd line of emplacements.	C.
	7th	1 A.M.	Artillery fairly quiet, a few 18 pounders could be heard. All guns were lain on their barrage lines by 2.45 A.M. including those that had up to that time been doing the usual harassing fire	C.
		3.10	A battery of field guns opened rapid fire 2 seconds or so before ZERO at which time 2 huge mines were exploded one on HILL 60 followed instantly by opening of artillery and M.G. barrage. Y one THE CATERPILLAR	
		3.11	Numerous enemy S.O.S. signals were seen.	
		3.12	Enemy artillery barrage commenced	
		4.40	J battery commenced to move forward reference ———	APPENDIX B
			by this time the hostile barrage had slackened	
		5.40	I battery commenced to move forward reference ———	APPENDIX B
				C.

Army Form C. 2118.

WAR DIARY
or
INTELLIGENCE SUMMARY.
(Erase heading not required.)

Instructions regarding War Diaries and Intelligence Summaries are contained in F. S. Regs., Part II. and the Staff Manual respectively. Title pages will be prepared in manuscript.

Place	Date	Hour	Summary of Events and Information	Remarks and references to Appendices
TRENCHES HILL 60 Sector	7th	5-2.30 am	The move forward was complete	C.
			Batches of prisoners were coming through and reports received that good progress was being made.	
		8.40 AM	The enemy barrage had practically ceased	
		10.A.M	Reported that the Black line was being consolidated	MAP A.
			No indication or signal of any counter attack was seen during the day or night	
			Fire was maintained on a line 200ˣ in advance of the Black dotted line on MAP "A"	
			Casualties 5. O.R. wounded	
			Rounds fired during 24 hours from ZERO approximately 37,500.	
	8		Day fairly quiet until about 2 p.m. when enemy artillery shelled neighbourhood of both "I" and "J" Battery positions without causing casualties	C.
			I Battery position was again shelled at 8 p.m. causing 3 casualties.	C.

Bentley Capt.

Army Form C. 2118.

WAR DIARY
or
INTELLIGENCE SUMMARY.
(Erase heading not required.)

Instructions regarding War Diaries and Intelligence Summaries are contained in F. S. Regs. Part II. and the Staff Manual respectively. Title pages will be prepared in manuscript.

Place	Date	Hour	Summary of Events and Information	Remarks and references to Appendices
	8		Enemy artillery became very active about 7 p.m. and at 8-15 p.m both batteries received S.O.S. and immediately opened fire on 4th barrage lines. Fire was continued for half an hour when situation cleared. At 8-45 p.m. both positions were again shelled causing 6 casualties.	A
	9	3.30 AM	"I" Battery fired 10,000 rounds at square J.31.A.4 (see MAP A) and square J.31.C.1. An enemy reported assembling in these places. Firing was carried on at intervals during the night on 4 barrage lines. Both battery positions were shelled at intervals. Approximately 77,000 rounds were fired. "I" Battery again shelled causing 1 casualty, 1 gun being destroyed by direct hit. Day fairly quiet. 4 guns of "I" Battery relieved 4 of 69 M.G. Company 2 in HILL 60 Crater and 2 in CATERPILLAR Crater. Relief complete 10-30 p.m. Remaining 4 guns "I" Battery withdrawn into reserve at MANOR FARM whole barrage frontage being taken over by "J" Battery who were held in readiness to fire on S.O.S.	B

Boulting Lieut

Army Form C. 2118.

WAR DIARY
or
INTELLIGENCE SUMMARY.
(Erase heading not required.)

Instructions regarding War Diaries and Intelligence Summaries are contained in F. S. Regs. Part II. and the Staff Manual respectively. Title pages will be prepared in manuscript.

Place	Date	Hour	Summary of Events and Information	Remarks and references to Appendices
	10th		Considerable artillery fire. Both HILL 60 & CATERPILLAR craters very heavily shelled	R
	11th	10.20 p.m. – 12 midnight	"J" Battery heavily shelled from 6 a.m. till 9 a.m. causing 13 casualties, "J" Battery therefore moved to "I" Battery positions, which were receiving less attention. HILL 60 crater shelled, causing 3 casualties.	R
		11.30 p.m.	Four guns in HILL 60 & CATERPILLAR craters relieved by 69 M.G. Coy & withdrawn into reserve at S.P.9.	R
	12th		Fairly quiet during day. Artillery active during night	R
	13th		Quiet.	R
	14th		At 7.30 p.m. our infantry carried out a local operation in BATTLE WOOD. Our guns were held in readiness to co-operate from Barrage positions, but their fire was not required.	R
	15th	2 a.m.	Company was withdrawn from the line. Shell fire was encountered on way out, causing 4 casualties. Personnel proceeded by Motor Lorry to Billets near THIEUSHOUK. Total casualties during operations (from ZERO hour) Killed 8, wounded 24, missing 1, wounded at duty 2.	R

Bombroy Lieut

Wt. W1422/M160 350,000 12/16 D. D. & L. Forms/C/2118/14.
A6945

WAR DIARY
or
INTELLIGENCE SUMMARY.
(Erase heading not required.)

Army Form C. 2118.

Place	Date	Hour	Summary of Events and Information	Remarks and references to Appendices
Nr THIELSHOUK	16		Overhauling of guns in Billets. 22 O.R. Reinforcements joined Company from Base.	R
	17		Company was inspected by G.O.C. Brigade near Billets. - Dress, Clemfrique	R
	18		A N.C.O. from the Gas School attended for the purpose of Refitting Box Respirators	R
	19/20		General Training near Billets	R
	21		Company was inspected by O.B. Dress - Battle Order	R
	22		Company practises with pack saddlery.	R
	23			
	24		General Training near Billets	R
	25			
	26		Company was inspected by G.O.C. Brigade - Drill Order	R
	27		Company proceeded to presentation of Medal Ribbons by G.O.C. Division	R
	28		A Range was alotted to the Company and a Lecture given in the afternoon	R
	29		Company inspected by G.O.C. Brigade Dress - Fighting Order	R
ZEVECOTEN CAMP	30	6.30am	Company left Billets and marched with Transport to ZEVECOTEN CAMP in reserve	R

Confidential

WAR DIARY

of

No. 68. Company

Machine Gun Corps

From 1st July 1917.
To 31st July 1917.

Army Form C. 2118.

WAR DIARY
or
INTELLIGENCE SUMMARY.
(Erase heading not required.)

Instructions regarding War Diaries and Intelligence
Summaries are contained in F. S. Regs., Part II.
and the Staff Manual respectively. Title pages
will be prepared in manuscript.

Place	Date	Hour	Summary of Events and Information	Remarks and references to Appendices
ZEVECOTEN CAMP	1919 July 1		In reserve at ZEVECOTEN CAMP.	Appx
	2		"	Appx
	3		"	Appx
	4		"	Appx
	5		"	Appx
MOUNT SORREL	6		This company relieved No. 70 Company M.G.C. in gun positions MOUNT SORREL – HILL 60 sector.	Appx
HILL 60 sector	7		In trenches.	Appx
	8		"	Appx
	9		"	Appx
	10		In trenches. 750 rounds fired at gaps in enemy wire during night	Appx
	11			Appx
	12		3000 rounds fired on enemy strong points in support of raid.	Appx
	13		2650 rounds were fired at enemy aircraft during the day. 1 O.R. killed. 2500 rounds fired on enemy aircraft	Appx
	14		In trenches.	Appx

A6945. Wt. W14422/M1160 350,000 12/16 D. D. & L. Forms/C./2118/14.

WAR DIARY
or
INTELLIGENCE SUMMARY.
(Erase heading not required.)

Army Form C. 2118.

Place	Date	Hour	Summary of Events and Information	Remarks and references to Appendices
	July 15		Relieved by 69 Company M.G.C. in early morning and went into reserve at ZEVECOTEN CAMP	Rfd.
	16		In reserve	Rfd.
	17		"	Rfd.
	18		"	Rfd.
	19		"	Rfd.
	20		Detachment of 4 officers & 63 OR with 8 guns relieved CORPS CAVALRY	Rfd.
	21		on aeroplane duty at ABEELE	Rfd.
	21		Company less detachment marched to billets near CAESTRE	Rfd.
	22		Training	Rfd.
	23		Training	Rfd.
	24		Inspected by G.O.C. Division	Rfd.
	25		Training	Rfd.
	26		"	Rfd.
	27			Rfd.
	28		Detachment at ABEELE relieved by detachment 70 Company M.G.C. and	Rfd.

WAR DIARY
or
INTELLIGENCE SUMMARY.
(Erase heading not required.)

Army Form C. 2118.

Place	Date	Hour	Summary of Events and Information	Remarks and references to Appendices
	July 29		Transport moved to EBLINGHEM	&c.
	30		Company proceeded by train from CAESTRE to S.t OMER & thence to billets at ESQUERDES. Transport completed the journey from EBLINGHEM to billets at ESQUERDES	&c. &c.
	31		Training	&c.

Kearney
Lt. Comdg. No. 68 Co. Machine Gun Corps.

Confidential

~~N° 68~~

War Diary

of

N° 68 Company

Machine Gun Corps.

From Aug 1st 1917
to Aug 31st 1917

WAR DIARY
or
INTELLIGENCE SUMMARY.

(Erase heading not required.)

Army Form C. 2118.

Instructions regarding War Diaries and Intelligence Summaries are contained in F. S. Regs., Part II. and the Staff Manual respectively. Title pages will be prepared in manuscript.

Place	Date	Hour	Summary of Events and Information	Remarks and references to Appendices
Esquerdes	Aug 1st		Company in Training	AR
	2		"	AR
	3		"	AR
	4		Two Sections firing on Range	AR
	5		"	AR
	6		Company in Training	AR
	7		Baths	AR
	8		Company firing on Range	AR
Salperwick	9		Company moved by Route March to SALPERWICK, transport moving with the Company	AR
	10		Route March with Pack Animals	AR
	11		Company in Training	AR
	12		"	AR
	13		Route March + Compass work	AR
	14		Company in Training	AR
	15		Tactical Scheme with Pack Animals	AR
	16		Field firing practise	AR

WAR DIARY
or
INTELLIGENCE SUMMARY.
(Erase heading not required.)

Army Form C. 2118.

Place	Date	Hour	Summary of Events and Information	Remarks and references to Appendices
SALPERWICK	Aug 17		Company in training	gR
	18		Route March with guns, tripods and ammunition on pack animals. 10 O.R. received instruction on FIRST AID	gR
	19		Cleaning guns etc.	gR
	20		Company Co-operated with Battalions in practising an attack	gR
	21		Company practised consolidating a position	gR
	22		Brigade Field Operations at field firing range. Company bivouacced at field firing range for night	gR
	23		Demonstration of covering fire to advancing troops	gR
	24	10.30 a.m.	Transport proceeded to OTTAWA CAMP arriving 10.30 p.m.	gR
	"	4.30 p.m.	Company proceeded by march to WATTEN arriving 6.15 pm. Entrained at WATTEN 1.30 a.m 25th arriving at RENINGHELST 8 a.m. + marched to OTTAWA CAMP.	gR
	26		Company in training	gR
	27		" " " 6 Guns reconnoitred of HOOGE Sector	gR
	28		" " "	gR
	29		Company moved to camp in DICKEBUSH area.	gR
	30		Company in training	gR
	31		" "	gR

M Donnell Rent for
O.C.omdg. No. 68 Co. Machine Gun Corps.

Confidential

War Diary

of

Nº 68 Coy. M.G.C.

From Sept 1st 1917

To " 30th "

WAR DIARY
INTELLIGENCE SUMMARY.
(Erase heading not required.)

Army Form C. 2118.
Page 70

Place	Date	Hour	Summary of Events and Information	Remarks and references to Appendices
DICKEBUSH area	1917 Sept 1		Company in training.	
	2		" "	
	3		Company proceeded by march to billets near STEENVORDE	
STEENVORDE area	4		Company in training.	
NOORDPEENE	5		Company proceeded by march to NOORDPEENE area (billets).	
"	6		Inspection by G.O.C. Brigade.	
"	7		Company in training	
"	8		" "	
"	9		" "	
"	10		" "	
"	11		" "	
"	12		" "	
"	13		Company proceeded by march to billets in STEENVORDE area.	
STEENVORDE	14		Company proceeded by march to CHIPPEWA CAMP near LA CLYTTE	
CHIPPEWA CAMP	15		Company in training.	
"	16		Company proceeded by march to camp near DICKEBUSH.	
DICKEBUSH	17		Company preparing to go into the line and for the part	

WAR DIARY
INTELLIGENCE SUMMARY.

Army Form C. 2118.

Page 7

Place	Date	Hour	Summary of Events and Information	Remarks and references to Appendices
DICKEBUSH	18		an offensive operations. Appendix "A" attached gives details of proposed operations. Reference map ZILLEBEKE 28 NW(4) + N.E.(3) Two Sections proceeded to TORR TOP tunnel	Appendix "A" p/w p/w
	19		In morning one of Sections remaining in camp proceeded to TORR TOP tunnel, the other (reserve Section) proceeding to BEDFORD HOUSE. At night the three Sections attached to assaulting troops (see appendix "A") moved out to the assembly positions, the reserve section moving up to TORR TOP tunnel.	p/w
TRENCHES	20		The attack was commenced at 5.40 am action of this Company appears from copy report attached as appendix "B". See appendix "B"	appendix "B" p/w p/w
	21		"	p/w
	22		"	p/w
	23		"	p/w
	24		Relieved by 100 + 116 Companies Machine Gun Corps and proceeded to Camp near BURGOMASTER FARM DICKEBUSH	p/w
	25		Company proceeded by motor lorry to WESTOUTRE	p/w

Comdg. No. 68 Co. Machine Gun Corps.

Army Form C. 2118.

Page 72

WAR DIARY
or
INTELLIGENCE SUMMARY.
(Erase heading not required.)

Place	Date	Hour	Summary of Events and Information	Remarks and references to Appendices
WESTOUTRE	26		Refitting and cleaning	Appx.
"	27		Refitting and training	Appx.
"	28		Company proceeded by march to Recce Camp	Appx.
WESTOUTRE				
"	29		Training	Appx.
"	30		Training	Appx.
			Total casualties during operations:-	
			Officers:- 1 killed, 2 wounded	
			O.R:- 9 killed, 16 wounded and 1 missing.	Appx.

Comdg. No. 68 Co. Machine Gun Corps.

APPENDIX "A"

Secret

Second Army Offensive

Brigade Plan of Operations

1. **GENERAL**

   (a) The X Corps is to be prepared to take part in an attack by the Second Army.
   Preparations for this attack are to be completed by Sept. 18th.

   (b) The X Corps will attack with three Divisions, 39th, 41st and 23rd in the order named from right to left.
   Two Divisions will be in corps reserve.

   (c) The 2nd Australian Division will be on the left of the 23rd Div.

   (d) The frontages & objectives allotted to the 23rd Division are shown on the attached map "A".

   THE OBJECTIVES ARE SHOWN AS FOLLOWS:

       1st OBJECTIVE — RED—
       2nd   "   BLUE—
       3rd   "   GREEN.

2. **ALLOTMENT OF TROOPS**

   (a) The 68th Infantry Brigade will attack on the front from JAVA AVENUE J.19.b.6.2 to junction JASPER DRIVE and GREEN JACKET RIDE J.19.b.7.7.

   (b) The 69th Inf. Bde. will attack on the front J.19.b.7.7 to JAR AVENUE J.19.c.2.9

   (c) The 70th Inf. Bde. will be in Divisional Reserve.

3. **ARTILLERY**

   (a) The attack of the 23rd Div. will be covered by five Brigades R.F.A. (1 as 1 Battery) organised in three groups, of which one group will be affiliated to the 68th Inf. Bde.

   (b) A barrage arranged in depth will cover the advance and will include all natures of Howitzers up to 9.2" (inclusive) in addition to the F.A. barrage.

   (c) The F.A. barrage will commence 150 yds. in advance of the front line of Infantry and will move forward at the following rate:-

To the RED LINE at rate of 100 yards in 8 minutes.
From RED to BLUE LINE at rate of 100 yds in 8 minutes
From BLUE to GREEN - - - - 100 yds in 10 "

(d) A pause of 30 minutes will be made after the RED objective is reached.

A pause of 1 hour 30 minutes after the BLUE objective is reached.

5. MACHINE GUNS

Four Machine Gun Coys. will be employed to form a machine gun barrage on the Div. front. Each Company will form two batteries of 8 guns. A group will consist of 4 batteries under a commander. A group Commander will be attached to the 88th Inf. Bde. H.Q.

The attack on the BLUE LINE will be covered by 4 batteries on the 88th Infantry Brigade front.

The attack on the GREEN LINE will be covered by 4 batteries on the 68th Infantry Brigade front, they will move forward for this purpose.

6. METHOD OF ATTACK

(a) The attack on the 3 objectives will be carried out by separate bodies of troops and each objective will at once be consolidated by the troops who have occupied it.

(b) Definite Units must be detailed to deal with known Strong points & to consolidate and garrison them when captured.

(c) Reserves will be sufficiently far forward to be in a position to reinforce the most advanced lines without delay.

7. MOPPING UP

Definite Units will be detailed to mop up specified Areas. These Units will be instructed to search thoroughly their areas for machine guns and they must ensure that no German capable of using his arms is overlooked, either in SHELL HOLES, DUGOUTS or elsewhere.

8. CONTACT PATROLS

A special party under the Command of 2/Lt. A.M. LYONS, 11th N.F. will meet a party of the 41st Division at J20.a.8.1.

(Continued)

CONTACT PATROLS (cont.)

A special party under the Command of 2/Lt. R.H. PENNEY. 11th N.F. will meet a party of 41st Division at J.20.d.2.9. This party will carry a pigeon, in order that a report of touch being obtained may be sent at once.

A special party under the Command of 2/Lt. G.C. WRIGHT, 13th D.L.I. will meet a party of the 41st Div. at TOWER HAMLETS. This party will also carry a pigeon.

Parties will also be detailed to meet parties of the 69th Inf. Bde. Meeting places will be notified later.

9. STRONG POINTS

Strong Points will be established at the following points:-

RED OBJECTIVE
A.   J.20.b.8.1.

BLUE OBJECTIVE
D.   Corner of Wood J.20.d.7.7.
E.   Dugouts   J.20.b.8.3½.
F.   KANTINTJE CABT. J.21.b.5.8.

GREEN OBJECTIVE
K   J.21.d.9½.8.
L   J.21.b.4.2.
M   J.21.b.9½.5.

10. R.E. and PIONEERS

R.E. and PIONEERS will be employed on the construction of STRONG POINTS. PIONEERS will mark out tracks V and W shown on Map "A" with posts marked with 2 white rings as early as possible. These tracks will be improved as opportunity offers.

13. ZERO hour will be notified later.

References to times will be in hours and minutes a.m. or p.m. and not as heretofore.

14 FORMATION FOR THE ATTACK

The attack on the RED LINE will be carried out by the 11th N.F. on the right, the 10th N.F. on the left.

The objectives will be as shewn on Map "A". The Dividing Line between Battalions in the attack on RED and BLUE objectives is shewn on MAP "A" by a GREEN LINE.

A Special Party will capture, consolidate and Garrison S.P. "A".

The attack on the BLUE LINE will be carried out by the 11th N.F. on right and 10th N.F. on the left.
Objectives and dividing line are as shewn on MAP "A".

The O.C. 11th N.F. will detail a Unit to capture, consolidate & garrison S.P. "D".

The O.C. 10th N.F. will detail a Unit to capture, consolidate & garrison S.P.s "E" & "F".

The attack on the GREEN LINE will be carried out by the 13th D.L.I.
Special parties will be detailed to deal with S.P.s "K", "L", & "M".

15 ASSEMBLY POSITIONS

The approximate positions of Battalions at ZERO HOUR on "ATTACK DAY" will be as follows:-

DIVISIONAL H.Q.	H.Q. Burgomaster Farm. H.34.c.o.i.
Brigade H.Q.	TORR TOP
10th N.F.	J.19.b.2.3
11th N.F.	J.19.b.o.2.
12th D.L.I.	TORR TOP
13th D.L.I.	TORR TOP

11th N.F. drawn up on tapes over trenches in J.19.b.
10th N.F.   "   "   "   "   "   "   "   "
12th D.L.I. W. of MAPLE TRENCH about J.24.c
13th D.L.I. in TORR TOP Subway

16. THE ATTACK

Every Company, Platoon, Section, must be given some special task, some special objective and some special task to do on reaching it.

Moppers up must be detailed to special areas and follow closely behind the assaulting troops. Carrying parties will carry all materials necessary for consolidation of the objective. Special parties will carry materials necessary for strengthening S.P. All carrying parties will follow as close behind the assaulting troops as possible. (see S.G. 153/3/1.)

The Attack on the RED LINE

At ZERO the 11th N.F. on the right and 10th N.F. on the left will advance and capture the RED LINE.

The 11th N.F. will be responsible for the capture, consolidation & garrison of Strong Point "A".

THE ATTACK ON THE BLUE LINE

At an hour to be notified later the 11th N.F. on the right and 10th N.F. on the left will advance from the RED LINE and capture the BLUE LINE.

The 11th N.F. will capture, consolidate and garrison S.P. "D". R.E. and PIONEERS will assist as soon as the situation allows.

The 10th N.F. will capture, consolidate & garrison S.P.s "E" & "F". R.E. & PIONEERS will assist in the construction of S.P. "E".

The Attack on the GREEN LINE

At an hour to be notified later the 13th D.L.I. will advance from the BLUE LINE & capture the GREEN LINE. They will be responsible for capturing, consolidating and garrisoning STRONG POINTS "K", "L" & "M".

19. O.P's

Brigade Observation Posts will be established at or near
J.14.c.2.1.
J.19.c.7.8.
prior to "ATTACK DAY"
After the capture of the GREEN LINE a forward O.P. will be established at a place to be selected by 2/Lt. R.A. MURRAY, B.I.O. at about J.21.a.5.2.

20. RUNNER ROUTES

Battalions will mark out runner routes as soon as possible after the advance from their Battalion H.Q. forward. These will be marked by small white sticks at frequent intervals.

The Brigade will lay out runner routes from Bde. H.Q. to Battn. H.Q. For this purpose, flags 2 feet sq. half black, half yellow will be used.

Similar flags 3 feet sq. will be used to mark relay posts. 2/Lt. F.J. BIDDULPH. R.E. B.S.O. will be responsible for marking Brigade runner routes.

21. Battalions will carry from Battalion forward dumps. The position & allocation of these, also their contents will be found in Instructions N° 9.

23. No papers dealing with this OPERATION will on any account be taken up to the line

Headquarters
68 Infantry Bde.

APPENDIX "B"

Reference Map
Zillebeke. 28 N.W.9 & N.E.3.
(parts of)

Reference your B.M.B. 16/43

The following is a short account of the attack on 20th inst. & subsequent operations

Dispositions

  1 Section (No 4) attached 11th N.F.
  1 Section (No 3)   "   10th N.F.
  1 Section (No 2)   "   13th D.L.I.
  1 Section (No 1) in reserve at Company H.Q.

Company H.Q. at TORR TOP.

Action of No 4 Section

This Section took up a position between 1 & 2 a.m. on the night 19th–20th Sept. just in rear of LUCKY DUGOUT. At Zero 2 guns under Lieut A. RAMSAY, which had been detailed for S.P. "A", went forward with the Infantry. The other 2 guns under Lieut. O. COULDREY went forward about 50 yards & took shelter in shell holes. The advance met with considerable opposition from a S.P. at about J.20.a.1.2. and three guns were brought into action against that S.P. Lieut RAMSAY was wounded here. His two teams however went forward under No 5520 Sgt NEWMAN. A. and got into position at S.P."A". Lieut COULDREY also went forward & took charge of them. The O.C. 11th N.F. decided to keep the other 2 guns in support & under his orders they were sent back to LUCKY DUGOUT. The teams at S.P.A. were subjected to heavy shell fire during attack & the following day. This shell fire became particularly intense on the evening of the 21st inst. At about 7. p.m. on 21st inst. an S.O.S. was observed from the Brigade on our right, & the guns in S.P."A" opened fire on enemy trenches on that front, some 2000 rounds being fired. At about 10 p.m. one gun was destroyed by a direct hit. At dawn on the 22nd inst. the dispositions of the Infantry having been modified and a defensive right flank formed, 1 gun was sent from LUCKY DUGOUT to S.P."D" covering the right flank, & the surviving gun at S.P. "A" withdrawn to LUCKY DUGOUT. This disposition, i.e. 1 gun at S.P. "D" & 2 at LUCKY DUGOUT, was continued till about 4.30 p.m. on 24th inst. when the guns were withdrawn.

ACTION of No 3 Section

This Section assembled at approximately J.19.b.9.3. At Zero the Section moved forward a few yards to avoid enemy barrage and waited till 10th N.F. advanced. Two guns under LIEUT. S.L. SMITH. then proceeded in direction of S.P. "F", one gun under No 12590 A/Sgt. ROBERTS. F. towards S.P. "E". & one gun under No 5519 Sgt. COLE. T towards S.P. "D". The two guns for S.P. "F" proceeded via JASPER DRIVE, (where casualties were suffered from M.G. fire, and one gun destroyed) and high ground near HERENTHAGE CHATEAU to neighbourhood of KANTINJE CABARET. After consultation with officer in charge of Infantry at S.P."F". gun was placed in position at about J.21.a.1.6. On account of casualties & loss of 1 gun. a gun & team complete was called for from Coy. H.Q. and arrived at about 1 p.m. This gun was placed in position at J.21.a.1.5. The gun for S.P."E" was taken forward by Sgt ROBERTS and placed in position in front of S.P."E". The gun team also placed in position and manned two captured German M.Guns. The gun for S.P. "D". was taken forward by Sgt. COLE & proceeded round the S. end of DUMBARTON LAKES & took up a position S. of S.P. "D". getting into action against enemy positions on TOWER HAMLETS ridge which appeared to be holding up advance on right. It then proceeded to S.P. "D" & got into position there. Casualties were sustained from sniping at this point. On the evening of 21st inst there was very heavy shelling by the enemy & S.O.S. went up on the front of the Brigade on the right. The right guns fired some 2,500 rounds on enemy positions on that front. Heavy shell fire was experienced on 22nd. 23rd (particularly at 7.30 p.m.) and 24th on evening of 24th inst. guns were withdrawn on line being taken over by No 116 M.G. Corps.

① No 8.

PROGRAMME for "I" and "J" BATTERIES

APPENDIX "B".

2/Lieut. R.G. THOMAS.

UNIT	TIME	TARGET	RATE OF FIRE	REMARKS
"I" & "J" Coy	Zero hrs to Z plus 30 minutes	Dotted Red line between points A – B	1 belt per gun per 4 minutes	
	Z plus Z/R Thro 30 minutes	Dotted Blue line between points A – B	1 belt per gun per 4 minutes	
("I") Batty (cont?)		Dotted BLUE line in front of "J" battery	1 belt per gun per 8 minutes	Fire to be maintained on the flanks whilst batteries are moving forward.
"J" Batty (cont?)		Dotted BLACK line	1 belt per gun per 8 minutes	
Both		Dotted BLACK line between points A & B	1 belt per gun per 4 minutes	

NOTE:-

At Zero hrs ..... "J" battery will move forward to J.2. position, and be in the new position by Z plus 2 hours 30 minutes. "I" battery will move forward to I.2 position by Z plus 3 hours 30 minutes.

Whilst the guns of the batteries are moving, fire will be maintained long range barrage target – keep up slow fire of 1 belt per gun per 8 minutes per gun for batten .... can between Dotted BLACK line between points A – B. Slow fire to be maintained ..... batteries at the half of 1 belt per gun per 8 minutes until dark, when long range .... fire may be ...... pure guns will be maintained at 20 minute intervals throughout the night by .... within the Zone .... S.O.S. are fired will be for ... than ....

.... per 10 minute, after 20 rounds a minute ....

At Zero plus 5 hrs. 30 mins. the barrage line will be lifted 200 yds in advance of the black dotted line in front covered by "I", "J", and 12th M.M.G. Batteries. In an emergency fire may be ordered within the above line.

Corrigenda to Brigade Instructions No 1
PLAN OF OPERATIONS

Para 14. Cancel and insert the following:

1. The attack on the RED LINE will be carried out by 11th N.F. The objective is as shewn in Operation Map "A", but there will be no dividing line between Battalions. A special unit will be detailed to capture, consolidate & garrison S.P. "A".

2. The attack on the BLUE LINE will be carried out by the 10th N.F., reinforced by two Companies of the 12th D.L.I. Owing to the apparently boggy nature of the ground in the DUMBARTON LAKE AREA, the 10th N.F. will advance as follows:

(a) Two companies will move on the general line of JAM LANE so as to be ready to advance from the line J.20.c.55-75 – J.20.2.56, at ZERO plus 1 hour 28 minutes. These two Coys. will follow in rear of the 122nd Inf. Bde, wheeling to their left as soon as they are clear of the Circular Lake in J.20.d. They will be responsible for clearing the area WEST of the BLUE LINE & SOUTH of a line from the building at J.21.a.05.15 to the track J.20.b.30.35.

(b) Two Coys. will move under the orders of the C.O.C. 69th Inf. Bde. via STIRLING CASTLE and HERENTHAGE CHATEAU so as to be ready to advance from a line between HERENTHAGE CHATEAU and the lake at J.20.b.80.95 in a S.E. direction by ZERO plus 1 hour 28 mins. These companies will be responsible for clearing the area WEST of the BLUE LINE & NORTH of the line J.21.a.05.15 – J.20.b.30.35.

(c) A Coy. of the 12th D.L.I. will follow each of the parties (a) and (b). These two Coys. are intended in the first place to form a reserve to the 13 D.L.I. in maintaining their hold on the GREEN LINE, and they will only be used to reinforce the 10th N.F. in case of necessity. Permission to do so should, if time permits, be obtained from A.11.B.Q.
These two Coys. will assemble on the line JASPER TR. J.30.b.50.45 [southwards]

(d) The O.C. 10th N.F. will detail parties to form & garrison the following Strong Points "D", "E" & "F".

3. The 23rd Div. Art. will keep a barage on the area J.20.b.50.45 – J.21.a.09.40 – J.20.b.80.00 – J.20.b.30.00, lifting off it from North to South in 3 successive lifts commencing at 1 hour 44 minutes and ending at 1 hour 52 minutes.

7. The 13th D.L.I. with one company of the 12 D.L.I. as a carrying party, will move so as to be in position to advance from the BLUE LINE at ZERO plus 4 hours 13 minutes.
Two Coys. of 13th D.L.I. with one Coy. of 12 D.L.I. will move South of the Circular Lake in J.20.d. & Two Coys. North of HERENTHAGE CHATEAU.
The O.C. 13th D.L.I. will be responsible for constructing & garrisoning S.P. "K", "L" & "M".

5. The improvement of the crossings of the stream joining the two western DUMBARTON LAKES will be undertaken by the 128th Field Coy. R.E. as soon as sufficient ground has been gained to cover working parties.

6. The O.Cs. 10th N.F. & 13th D.L.I. will send on parties to reconnoitre the way previous to the time selected for their advance. These parties will return & act as guides.

MACHINE GUNS.

1. The attack will be supported by a machine gun barrage.
2. The 19th M.G.Coy. + 248th M.G.Coy. will cover the advance of the 68th Inf. Bde.
    They will form —
    19th M.G.Coy. "A" and "B" Batteries 8 guns each.
    248th " "   "C" and "D"   "   "   "   "
    19th   " "   will form No 6 group.
    248th " "   "   "   No 7   "
3. Major. G.S. HUTCHISON, M.C. will command Nos 6+7 groups, and will be attached to the 68th Infantry Brigade.
4. Nos 6+7 groups will move forward to support the 3rd Objective.
5. ~~The barrage table~~
6. (a) Rate of fire while supporting the attack will be 1 belt per gun per 4 mins.
   (b) "   " "   during intervening periods,   " "   "   "   " " 8 mins.
7. Rate of fire for S.O.S. Signals will be 1 belt per gun per 2 minutes, for 10 minutes. Afterwards until situation is clear 20 rnds. per minute.
8. All guns employed on the Div. Barrage can be turned on any part of the front.
11. One gun in each battery is allotted for anti-aircraft work. It will fire in the barrage but will be withdrawn as required.
12. 68th M.G.Coy.
    Guns of the 68th M.G.C. are allotted as follows :-
    4 guns under LIEUT. S.L. SMITH, to 10th N.F.
    4 "   "   LIEUT. O. COULDREY to 11th N.F.
    4 "   "   LIEUT. J.A. DOMMETT to 13th D.L.I.
    { Guns allotted to Units will be used by C.O.s of Battalions to garrison strong Points. They may also be used in the attack at the C.O.s discretion.
13. O.C. 68 M.G.C. will be with S.B.H.Q. in ~~a dug-out about Tip.85.95~~ TORR TOP tunnel. The 4 guns in reserve will be at TORR TOP and remain there until required.

4 guns in Bde. Reserve under Lieut. R.G. WILLIAMS.

Artillery Arrangements

Ref. Brigade Plan of Operations. PARA. 3. c + d. will be amended in accordance with these instructions

2. The Infantry will halt on the 1st (RED) objective for 3/4 hour (45 mins) and on the 2nd (BLUE) objective for two hours approximately. Infantry posts will be pushed forward a maximum distance of 100 yds. in front of the final line selected for consolidation.

3. The movements of the barrage will be as follows:-

TO RED LINE

At Zero the barrage will come down at the safety limit (about 150 yards) in front of our front line, where it will remain until Zero plus 3 mins. whilst the Infantry close up to it.

At Zero plus 3 mins. the barrage moves forward covering the first two hundred yards at 100 yards in 4 minutes & then slowing down to 100 yards in 6 minutes till it is 200 yards beyond the RED LINE where it pauses.

TO BLUE LINE

The barrage will advance at the rate of 100 yds in 8 minutes.

TO GREEN LINE

The barrage will advance at the rate of 100 yds. in 8 minutes and the protective barrage will be found 200 yds beyond the green line.

4. The dividing line for barrage purposes between the 23rd Division & 1st Australian Div. is a line through J15.d.30.78 - J14.c.47.98.

POINTS	Beyond RED LINE	
	Barrage reaches + pauses.	Barrage resumes advance
Line c J.20.d.20.92.	Zero plus 35 mins	Zero plus 1 hr. 28 minutes
" d J.114.d.93.86.	" " 35 "	" " " " "
	BEYOND BLUE LINE	
Line c J.21.c.10.86.	Zero plus 1hr. 52 mins.	" " ~~52'~~ 4 hrs 15 m
" d J.15.c.83.80.	" " " " "	" " " " "
	BEYOND GREEN LINE	
Line c J.21.d.52.75.	Zero plus 5 hrs. 3 mins.	} remain as protective
" d J.15.d.70.77.	" " 4 hrs. 49 mins	} Barrage

5. The Infantry will be notified when they reach the RED, BLUE and GREEN lines respectively by firing a proportion of smoke shells in the barrage.

ACTION of No 2 Section

This Section assembled in Front of 13th D.L.I., 2 guns under Lt DOMMETT on right, and 2 under 2/Lt R.F. SMITH on left.

These guns moved forward with the 13th D.L.I. 2/Lt SMITH was however killed & casualties caused to his gun teams before they reached our original front line. No 5483 Sgt COOPER.C. collected the survivors of the teams & moved forward, joining Lt DOMMETT. The Section then moved forward with 13th D.L.I. getting into action on the BLUE LINE against enemy S.P.s which were resisting. The green line was reached about 11.15 a.m. and all 4 guns came into action at about J.21.b.1.0. against enemy S.P.s & positions on front of Brigade on our right which appeared to be held up. The MENIN Rd & ground S. of it was also covered. During the day several casualties were caused by sniping & M.G. fire, Lt DOMMETT being wounded. One gun was knocked out. At dark when it became possible to move about Sgt COOPER (who was then in charge) reconnoitred the position situation & discovering that the dugouts at J.21.b.2.1. were only held by 5 men of the 13.D.L.I. & that this position seemed to be an important one capable of defence by M. Guns, he moved his three guns there, also mounting 2 captured German guns. This position was retained until the teams were relieved by No 1 Section on the 22nd inst.

ACTION of No 1 Section

This Section was in reserve at TORR TOP under Lt. R.G. WILLIAMS. At about 10.30 a.m on the 20th inst. orders were received to send up 1 gun to S.P."F" to replace guns destroyed. One team with gun, tripod & ammunition complete was sent up under Lt. R.G. WILLIAMS, reaching S.P. "F" without casualty. This gun was placed in position at J.21.a.1.5. & handed over to LIEUT. S.L. SMITH.

On 22nd inst. No 1 Section's remaining 3 guns with teams were sent up to the GREEN LINE under Lt. R.G. WILLIAMS to relieve No 2 Section. Relief was completed without casualty. Disposition of guns were slightly altered, 1 gun being withdrawn to dugout at J.21.a.9.3. where it could cover the MENIN Rd. & also be moved readily to meet an attack from any direction.

The position at J.21.b.2.1 was defended by 1 Vickers gun & 1 German gun at J.21.b.2.1. covering the MENIN Rd. & also capable of supporting the Infantry N. of the Road. One Vickers gun was placed at J.21.b.2.0. covering GHELUVELT & the ridge South of that Village & also capable of firing S.E. down the valley at J.21.d. A German gun was placed at J.21.b.2.0. firing S.W. and covering the German S.P. & positions on the right flank about J.21.d.1.7. On relief of 13th D.L.I. by 8th K.O.Y.L.I. 3 bombers were obtained from latter as an escort for M. Guns to replace 5 men of 13 D.L.I and a listening post established about 30 yds in front of J.21.b.2.1.

Heavy shell fire was experienced on the 23rd inst. from 4 to 6 a.m, & on the 24th inst about 5 a.m. About 2000 rnds were fired (principally from the German guns) on the enemy positions during these bombardments. At 9.15 p.m on the 23rd inst. an enemy patrol of 3 men was fired on, one of the men being wounded & subsequently brought in. He died within ½ an hour however. At 5.20 p.m on the 24th inst. 2 Germans approached the position & took cover in some ruins in front. They were cut off by our M.G. fire & surrendered to a small party organized from the gun teams to fetch them in. Apparently they had lost their way. They were handed over to O.C. "B" Coy 8th K.O.Y.L.I. to be sent to the rear under escort. At 6.30 p.m on the same day 200 rounds were fired on the enemy - about 20 strong - seen moving about in GHELUVELT. It is believed that casualties were inflicted.

At 9. p.m on the 24th inst. 2 guns were relieved by 100 M.G. Coy & one by 116 M.G. Coy.

Comdg. No. 89 Coy. Machine Gun Corps.

No 68 Coy. M.G.C.

Confidential

War Diary

From Oct 1st 1917
To   Oct 31st 1917.

WAR DIARY
or
INTELLIGENCE SUMMARY.

(Erase heading not required.)

Army Form C. 2118.

Page 73

Place	Date	Hour	Summary of Events and Information	Remarks and references to Appendices
	1917 Oct 1		Company proceeded by march to hutments near BERTHEN	P/W
	2		Company proceeded by march to billets near THIEUSHOUCK	P/W
THIEUSHOUCK	3		Training	P/W
	4		Training	P/W
	5		Training	P/W
	6		Training	P/W
	7		Company proceeded by march to ASCOT CAMP WESTOUTRE	P/W
	8		Training	P/W
WESTOUTRE	9		Company proceeded by motor bus to camp near DICKEBUSH.	P/W
	10		Preparing for line.	P/W
	11		Company relieved part 220 Machine Gun Company and that 22 Machine Gun Company in the line E. of POLYGON DE ZONNEBEKE. Dispositions - 7 guns in front system, 2 guns in barrage positions, 2 in close reserve at Inverness, Company H.Q. 5 in reserve at Maneparr lines	P/W
	12		Heavy shellfire was experienced during	P/W

WAR DIARY
or
INTELLIGENCE SUMMARY.
(Erase heading not required.)

Army Form C. 2118.

Page 74

Place	Date	Hour	Summary of Events and Information	Remarks and references to Appendices
	12		Two guns being destroyed and one close reserve gun sent forward to replace same the other being withdrawn to reserve. Casualties - 2 O.R. killed 1 O.R. missing believed killed 5 O.R. wounded.	P/W
	13		In position	P/W
	14		Two reserve guns placed in barrage positions	P/W
	15		1000 rounds fired into BECELAERE during night.	P/W
	16		Relieved by 194 Machine Gun Company and proceeded by march to camp near CHATEAU SEGARD (ANZAC CAMP)	P/W
	17		Cleaning	P/W
	18		No. 3 Section with 4 guns moved up to CLAPHAM JUNCTION in Brigade reserve.	
	19		Cleaning and training	P/W
	20		Company less No. 3 Section (in Brigade reserve and number 1 & 2 sections which attached to 194 Company) and number 1 & 2 sections which were attached to 70 Machine Gun Company for duty with ...	P/W

Comdg. No. 68 Co. Machine Gun Corps.

Army Form C. 2118.

WAR DIARY
or
INTELLIGENCE SUMMARY.
(Erase heading not required.)

Page 75

Place	Date	Hour	Summary of Events and Information	Remarks and references to Appendices
	21		7th Division entrained at VLAMERTINGHE 11 p.m., detrained at WIZERNES at 6 am 22nd and proceeded by march to billets in VAL D'ACQUIN.	
	22nd		Cleaning	R/W
	23		Training	R/W
	24		Training	R/W
	25		Inspection and presentation of Medal ribbons by G.O.C. Division	R/W
	26		Training	R/W
	27		Training	R/W
	28		Nos 1 and 2 sections rejoined the Company	R/W
	29		Inspection of Brigade by Brigadier and G.O.C. Division	R/W
	30		Baths cleaning and refitting	R/W
	31		Inspection of Brigade by Commander in Chief.	R/W

M. Sumner t/c
Comdg. No. 68 Co. Machine Gun Corps.

www.ingramcontent.com/pod-product-compliance
Lightning Source LLC
Chambersburg PA
CBHW081549160426
43191CB00011B/1874